Shivaji

and His Swarajya Adventures

Leadership Lessons for Young Indians

Janhavi Samant loves telling stories. As a journalist, she told stories about Mumbai and its people. Then she authored *Faaltugiri and Other Flashbacks*, a book narrating funny stories from her childhood, and later *When Elephants Had Wings & Other Funny Stories*. Today, she is a digital marketing professional who creates content around brands.

As a child, Janhavi would hear many tales—some funny, some heroic, some tragic and some downright disgusting—from her grandmom and parents. As a mom, she loves retelling, recycling and even making up a few stories for her own kids at bedtime. She believes stories build bonds between parents and kids. Besides, they are the easiest way to imagine ourselves in a different place.

The wise say that those who tell stories rule the world. So, Janhavi is getting ready to rule this world!

Published by Red Panda, an imprint of Westland Books, a division of Nasadiya Technologies Private Limited, in 2025

No. 269/2B, First Floor, 'Irai Arul', Vimalraj Street, Nethaji Nagar, Alapakkam Main Road, Maduravoyal, Chennai 600095

Westland, the Westland logo, Red Panda and the Red Panda logo are the trademarks of Nasadiya Technologies Private Limited, or its affiliates.

ISBN: 9789360451417

10 9 8 7 6 5 4 3 2 1

Printed at Nutech Print Services, India

SHIVAJI

AND HIS SWARAJYA ADVENTURES

JANHAVI SAMANT

Illustrated by Charbak Dipta

Dedicated to Jijabai and all the mothers who believe in the greatness of their children.

प्रजानां विनयाधानाद्रक्षणाद्भरणादपि।
स पिता पितरस्तासां केवलं जन्महेतवः।।

It is the one who protects, nurtures and takes responsibility for his people who is the real father.
The one who gives birth is just incidental

- Poet Kalidasa

Contents

Chapter 1

The Birth of a King

'Shivba ... Shivaji!'

She softly whispered into the baby's ears. The infant's eyes met his mother's and the tiny face broke into a smile. At the temple in the Shivneri fort in Junnar, where her son was born, Jijabai bowed respectfully in front of Maa Shivbai Devi and looked into the benevolent eyes of the family deity that had blessed generations of the Bhonsle clan.

With the blessings of Maa Shivbai Devi, her son would be a strong, brave warrior and a fair and just leader. She named him after the Goddess for answering her prayers. Jijabai vowed that her son would make her proud, before anointing his head with a vermillion *tikka* from the feet of the Goddess. Jijabai's Shivba would eventually prove her right.

It was 1630. The world came to know this child, Shivba, as the Great Maratha Warrior—Chhatrapati Shivaji Maharaj—

the first person to dream of Hindavi Swarajya. He dared to envision a kingdom that would shrug off the yoke of Adil Shahi, Ahmed Shahi and the Mughal rulers who had created insecurity, mistrust and instability in the region and among the people, due to their power mongering. Shivba aspired for a state that would care for its people—a land that would belong to the people. It was a vision that took root in Shivba's heart at a young age, and he dedicated his entire life to turning it into reality. Shivshahi, his rule, continued to be a legacy for India and was the guiding light in our struggle for Swarajya against British rule, several decades later.

Jijabai Bhonsle was a strong, proud and independent warrior woman. Hailing from the Jadhav family of Sindkhed Raja, Jijabai was the daughter of Lakhuji and Mhalsabai. Lakhuji was a proud Maratha sardar serving in the army of the Ahmednagar Sultanate. In those days, girls were not allowed to study or become soldiers. But that did not stop young Jija.

Despite being self-taught, Jija was extremely skilled at horse riding and sword fighting. She was also an observant child. With a sharp mind, she learnt a lot about military planning, the rules of the *jagirdari* and land revenue system and politics just from observing discussions between her father and brothers.

At a young age, perhaps when she was only fourteen or fifteen, she was married off to Shahaji Bhonsle, another Maratha warrior from Verul village in Maharashtra. Shahaji was a sardar serving Nizam Shah. Jijabai had spent enough years in a household full of proud Maratha warriors to truly understand the unpredictability of that life. Her father or husband would

often have to leave at a moment's notice to fight battles with unknown enemies at just a click of their feudal masters' fingers.

At the time—more than four hundred years ago—the world around young Jijabai was one of chaos and instability. The Indian subcontinent was fragmented with many weak, indulgent and short-sighted kings who kept fighting amongst themselves over petty causes. Many of them went bankrupt due to lavish, indulgent lifestyles. They were corrupt enough to then allow foreign powers to slowly usurp their rights and their treasuries, even as their subjects suffered helplessly.

The Sardars lived and fought in risky conditions while the kings who ordered them around led extravagant lives. They fought to protect the royalty; extorted taxes from their own people and looted enemy lands to fill the treasuries of their masters. Their masters, however, chose to fight or surrender when it suited them without a care for the soldiers who were laying their lives down for the kingdom. Jijabai's father and husband had dedicated themselves to these fierce, violent lives. Her elder son, seven-year-old Sambhaji, Shivba's older brother, was already being groomed to become a warrior.

This time around, right from pregnancy, Jijabai had been determined to be more in control of this baby's future. On those quiet mornings at Shivneri fort, she would pray to Goddess Shivai for another strong, brave son who would have the strength and courage to not only rule over his own people but also take responsibility for their safety and well-being. She prayed that the blessed land of the Marathas would find a new leader who would usher its people to prosperity.

It wasn't like Mother Nature had blessed her country either. The Maharashtra that Jijabai grew up in was a harsh, unforgiving region. The population was sparse and living conditions were difficult. Thick forests covered much of the western edge of the Deccan plateau and rainfall was low and uncertain. Farmers and labourers made a meagre living, with rice cultivation being impossible. Their staple was millets, but only if rainfall was consistent. Some years just passed in drought and poverty. The land was formed around the districts of Nasik, Poona, Satara and a few regions of Ahmednagar, Solapur and the western parts of Aurangabad. The Marathas were settled in this belt between the Western Ghats and the Arabian Sea. Very few people spoke Marathi in the form we know it today, too.

The rough and rocky terrain overrun with forests made travelling very difficult. There was no way—unless you were a skilled horse rider—to go from one province to another, either for pleasure or shopping or exploring. There were no busy or popular trade centres that people could visit. The terrain had carved up the land into several small, independent units and people lived fairly isolated lives. The region was frequented only by traders and businessmen from the Arab and European

Mahatma Jyotiba Phule researched the legend of Shivaji Maharaj and compiled a book on him, *A Ballad on Shivaji*. He also recorded all the *powadas*, long poems glorifying the life and works of the Maharaj. He later used the powadas to promote the ideals of Shivaji Maharaj to spread the idea of social justice and literacy in the Maharashtrian society.

world who visited the ports on the western coast to buy textiles, metals and spices to take back home.

The sole advantage of this isolation was, of course, natural protection from foreign invaders. Many foreign rulers from the north and south—Hindus and Muslims—who tried to seize this land, ended up badly defeated. Mostly by the terrain itself but also by the fierce locals who were the only ones who knew how to navigate the steep hills and mountains, thick-walled and high forts and thorny forests. It allowed the region to be naturally well-protected and resilient to long battles, if required. This was also how these fierce Maratha sardars ended up getting recruited by the Sultanates to wage wars in other regions in return for *jagirs.* Jagirs were land parcels bestowed on brave soldiers as a reward. The soldiers were in charge of the administration of such land parcels, had to collect taxes from the land tillers on behalf of the King and keep a portion of such collections as their earnings. Such administrators were called jagirdars or subedars.

But Jijabai knew that this natural reprieve wouldn't last long. The Mughals wanted a foothold in the Deccan and were constantly in a tussle with the Islamic Sultanates of Bijapur, Golconda and Ahmednagar that controlled most parts of Maharashtra. The Portuguese and Dutch forces had been fighting for power closer home, and it seemed that the English had started to enter this fray. She knew that although her land was safe from Indian kings, they were vulnerable to the Portuguese, Dutch and English adversaries because of their huge sea armies and naval super-prowess, with which they were ruling over the entire world. She knew that the geopolitical situation around their region was getting riskier by the day. And if the Marathas did not take this danger seriously, they would have to forever accept a life of slavery and bondage.

The times were changing and it was time for the Marathas to change as well.

It was time for the proud warriors to find a good leader who would protect them and take responsibility for them, she thought.

'Shivba ... Shivaji! It is time.' She whispered softly in the baby's ears once again.

Chapter 2

Growing Up At Shivneri

Right from the time of little Shivba's birth, Jijabai was determined to ensure that the infant lived a safe, secure life, so that he could learn about his motherland and how to protect his people.

Her husband, Shahaji, lived an adventurous life, constantly moving from one battle camp or enemy territory to another in the early years of his second son's life. This didn't seem to be the best environment to bring up a child. Jijabai, therefore, decided early on to stay back at Shivneri with Shivaji and bring him up in the predictable routine of village life in that secure stronghold.

Consequently, Jijabai and Shivba lived a quiet, more or less isolated, life of solitude in the company of a few loyal soldiers and their families. Jijabai would spend considerable time taking care of administrative work around the fort. The rest of her time was dedicated to spiritual pursuits and raising her son. Little Shivba had no friends or companions in these early years and it fell on Jijabai to be a companion, playmate as well as nurturer to the young mind.

In her pursuit to acquaint Shivba with his culture and motherland, Jijabai began mentoring the child early on. From a very young age, Jijabai pushed her son to play outdoors. With a watchful eye, she would encourage the boy to climb trees and describe the view from the treetops. This was so that he learnt to watch out for movements in the jungle and people entering the fort. Under her supervision, the wiry young boy would learn to trek in the woods and identify shrubs, small plants and animals. Far from being scared, Shivba would often rush to pick up a rat or frog or lizard; look at it closely and then set it free. Once when she saw the lonely boy gather wooden sticks to use as fake knives and swords, she allowed him to look at and touch a real sword. She was amused to see her little one in awe of a shining sword. She saw him run his hand gently up and down the sword and said, 'Someday, Ma Bhavani will give you a divine sword of your own, which you will use to protect your motherland.'

She would also often take her young son for kirtans and bhajans—devotional songs about gods and goddesses and poetry by saints from the Bhakti Movement, such as Gora Kumbhar or Dnyaneshwar or Chokha Mela—that would often end in spiritual sermons about true spirituality and humanity.

Jijabai had a truly liberal mindset and interacted with and subscribed to the spiritual learnings of many Hindu and

Muslim saints and gurus of all castes. This quality was instilled in Shivaji at a very young age.

Since she herself was not literate, she relied on the spiritual learnings of Indian culture and mythology, and its epic tales of courage, bravery and wisdom, to begin Shivaji's education.

It can be said that young Shivaji grew up in the company of epic heroes like Rama, Krishna or the Pandavas, learning about their childhoods, sacrifices, as well as battles and military strategy. He also heard many stories of the courage of Kali Ma and Durga and their legendary fights. Jijabai and her son's days were spent in this imaginary world. When Jijabai was not narrating these stories to Shivba, she would be watching him enact these epics, complete with imaginary fight sequences.

Sometimes, he would take a rope and pretend to be young Krishna fighting the snake demon Kaalia. He would jump off his bed, as if he were jumping into the Yamuna, swim and wrestle with the rope, and emerge victorious. Sometimes, he would pretend that it was the Vaishampayan lake. He would then become Bheem who had been drugged and pushed into that magical lake by Duryodhana.

Some afternoons, Jijabai would return from her siesta to find that her *matki* (earthen pot) of butter, hanging from the ceiling,

Leadership Lesson #1

Listen to the whole story. Look at the whole picture. Only then decide on your course of action. Do not act on half information.

had been emptied of all its contents, or that milk was spilt across the kitchen or discover tiny handprints on the jaggery container. Shivba had turned into Yashoda's young Krishna.

Some evenings she would return from her evening prayers to find furniture and household knickknacks arranged in a spiral loop. Shivba was fighting imaginary Kauravas as he pretended to be Abhimanyu—the young brave warrior son of the Pandavas—who was killed as he valiantly tried to escape the *chakravyuh.*

'Why did Abhimanyu enter the *chakravyuh* without fully learning how to escape it? Why could he not be patient?' Shivba would ask his mother. 'Because he acted on half information. In battle, it is important to act only after you have all the facts in place. Sometimes, discretion is the better part of valour,' Jijabai would answer patiently.

She took every opportunity to talk about the qualities she wanted to inculcate in her young son. Shivba's intelligent mind soaked up these stories like a sponge and this fantasy world of his childhood formed the core of the young boy's value system. He was unable to accept injustice in any form.

'*Aaisaheb*, why was Eklavya forced to cut off his thumb? It was so unfair. Couldn't Dronacharya have taught him alongside the Pandavas and Kauravas?' an outraged Shivaji asked Jijabai as he lay on her lap before bedtime.

'Shivba, life is often unfair for the underprivileged because of the actions of the powerful. The Kauravas of Hastinapur were too blind to the injustice that was perpetrated by their *rajguru* (royal teacher). Such small transgressions by the Kauravas and their loyalists brought down that whole kingdom. It is the duty of a king to right the wrongs done to his people,' Jijabai would explain gently as she ruffled the young boy's hair.

When Shivaji made friends with young kids around the fort, Jijabai often found them jumping up and down the hills, swinging on trees and enacting battles from the Mahabharata and Ramayana. Or he would be holding imaginary court, listening to his friends' imaginary problems and offering solutions.

Many evenings were spent in discussing moral dilemmas arising out of these epic stories. 'Why did the Pandavas wait so long to take revenge on the Kauravas for Draupadi's *vastraharan*?' he would ask agitatedly.

'What would you have done Shivba?' Jijabai would ask.

'You say that women are to be respected, always. I would have immediately cut off Dushshasan and Duryodhana's hands for wrongly touching a woman's saree,' he would quickly say.

'That would be the right thing for a king to do. When justice is administered, it has to be timely as well as effective as a deterrent. When criminals disrespecting women are not dealt with, it creates a precedent for others to mistreat women as well. A king's duty is to set an example through the

Leadership Lesson #2
Battles need to be first won in the mind before they can be won physically. Believe in what you are fighting for.

punishment he metes out so that others will be discouraged from perpetrating such crimes,' Jijabai would say.

Through every story, young Shivaji was learning important leadership lessons that would hold him in good stead for when he would assume charge of his motherland. Jijabai would talk to him about how important it was for a leader to have vision, to think ahead of the enemy and to always be prepared for all emergencies. She would also always emphasise on the value of information and communication in military strategy.

'Why did the Pandavas spread the rumour that the great Kaurava warrior, Ashwatthama, was killed in battle? Wasn't it a mean trick to play?' he would ask.

'Ashwatthama was Guru Dronacharya's son. The Pandavas knew that the news of the loss of his son would weaken the *rajguru* and his army. The Pandavas could then immediately launch an offensive that would weaken them further. All is fair in love and war, they say. The Pandavas did this to get an emotional advantage over the Kaurava forces. Sometimes, the battle has to be fought with the enemy's mind rather than on the ground,' she would answer.

Leadership Lesson #3

A leader always needs to be prepared for all eventualities.

Mother and son continued to be close until her death. Later in life, even after he became king, Shivaji was known to rely on his mother's advice and moral compass for making important policy decisions.

Young Shivba lived with Jijabai in Shivneri till he turned six or seven years old, after which they went to live in Poona where the pre-adolescent Shivba was to start some of the great adventures of his life.

Chapter 3

Shivba Moves to Poona

When Shivaji was six or seven, Shahaji had to surrender Shivneri and a few other forts to the Mughals in return for peace. He kept with him his *jagir* of Poona, where Jijabai and Shivaji were brought and settled. Shahaji appointed Dadaji Konddev to administer the estate and then moved back to Bijapur to take up his official responsibilities in the court of Adil Shah.

At the time, the Poona estate was in shambles and running into tremendous losses. The area was ravaged by constant battles, a recent famine and looted repeatedly by opportunists. The province had changed hands between the Nizam and Adil Shah multiple times before any ruler could take proper charge of it and implement any lasting changes. Besides this, wild wolves had been descending from the hills, attacking residents and flattening the fields.

The province needed a strong administrator who could tackle these problems and create stability in the region. It was the only way for the estate to become a source of revenue for the *jagir*. Dadaji Konddev proved to be the best man for the job. He quickly took charge of the affairs in Poona.

He got the villagers to kill the wolves for monetary rewards and then geared them to start cultivating the land with subsidies from the *jagir*. Needless to say, Jijabai and Shahaji both saw Dadaji's influence on Poona as a positive one and decided that he should also oversee young Shivaji's training in administration as well as military skills. Thus started Shivba's formal training.

In his Shivneri days, the young lad was mostly left to his own devices with little or no discipline. He had run wild in the forests, climbed trees and lived more or less a lonely existence. He had been the master of his own time and hobbies. Infact, it would not be an exaggeration to say that Shivba had a mind of his own and wasn't too amenable to taking instructions from anyone.

Nevertheless he was a quick learner, effortlessly absorbing physical skills like a sponge. But, apart from that, formal training turned out to be a challenge for him. He had to wake up early in

Leadership Lesson #4

A leader's strength and power are derived from their discipline and decision-making. An indecisive leader will never be able to take care of their people.

the morning, follow rules and regulations, learn and memorise stuff and, more importantly, obey his teachers.

'*Aaisaheb*, why do I have to ride the horse in that particular way only? Why can't I ride him the way I have taught myself? I can ride better than this teacher,' a disgruntled Shivba would tell his mother.

'Riding for pleasure is very different from riding in a battle, Shivba. It not only requires skill but also practice and right body language. If you want to learn something, you need to be humble. Bend your head down and listen to what your teacher is saying. Do you want to go into a battle with only half the knowledge, like Abhimanyu?' Jijabai would warn her son.

Shivba did see the sense in that. And, usually, his mother always gave him good advice. So, while he became slightly more patient with his tutors, he was unable to fully control his unruly, independent spirit. At times, he would ignore the riding tutor's instructions and rush off into the forests further ahead than he should have. Sometimes, he would go so far ahead that he would return home only in the evening, having missed all the classes of the day.

The worst thing, according to him, was to study indoors with books. He just couldn't settle. Jijabai would get constant complaints from his tutors.

'Shivba, you cannot run away from your teacher like this. He takes a lot of effort to help you with your lessons. If you want to become a leader of the people, you need to learn how to work for them,' she would reprimand him.

'*Aaisaheb*, a leader has to be brave and take care of his subjects. I am brave and will fight for my country and its people. But please do not ask me to learn from books,' Shivaji would plead.

Jijabai was at her wits' end getting her son to study. Dadaji Konddev also tried his best to encourage Shivaji to enjoy books, reading and writing. He would often make the lad attend his administrative meetings, discussions on revenue and book-keeping. Young Shivaji liked to meet people, especially from his estate, and interact with them. He was a natural problem-solver who came up with creative solutions to local issues and enjoyed these administrative meetings. However, he would never be interested enough to be involved in routine procedural work around the estate.

Observing his complete disinterest in learning anything academic, Dadaji Konddev often counselled him as well. 'Don't you want to run a *jagir*? Become a brave sardar of the Sultanate like your father?' he would ask.

Shivaji would reply boldly, 'I will be my own ruler. I will fight for my own land and people, not for anybody else.'

Initially, Dadaji thought that these were just naïve, bold claims of a young lad. But as Shivba grew into an adolescent,

Leadership Lesson #5
Pardoning a deliberate act of crime makes a leader appear weak in front of their people. Rules are meant to be followed by everyone.

Dadaji knew that his independent spirit would never bend to anyone's will. There was an incident that proved this more than any words ever could.

Once Jijabai and Shivaji went to Bijapur to meet with his father. Shahaji was very deeply moved to see his son after so many years, all grown up now. He proudly took Shivba to the palace and offices of the Sultanate to introduce him to his colleagues. Shivba was also impressed looking at the authority that his father wielded with the other officers of the Bijapur court. When returning to their living quarters, Shahaji promised, 'Tomorrow, I will take you to meet Adil Shah in his court.'

The next day, Shahaji got his teen son ready and took him to Adil Shah's court. Shivba was awed to see the pomp and splendour. He stood with his father in the court. He was amazed to see several other sardars like Shahaji. When the king arrived in court, he too rose up like his father and the other officers. He noticed that everyone in court was bowing down low in a *maanacha mujra* in front of the king with deference. He was surprised to see his father do the same. But Shivaji didn't bow down. He just stood there with his head bowed.

Shahaji nudged his son and whispered, 'Shivba, bow before the king. Show him respect.'

Shivba looked up at his father and said, 'He is not my king. I refuse to bow before him.'

Shahaji reiterated, 'He is our master. He is the one who has granted us our estate. We need to show him utmost respect.'

Shivba was aware of having displeased his father. He was also aware that other court officers were watching this interaction.

Some of them were whispering to him to bow down too. He felt apologetic but he refused to relent. It is said that Adil Shah noticed the young lad who did not formally curtsy before him. He was miffed with this attitude but decided to let it go for the moment. After all, he was a young boy and couldn't do him any harm.

It turns out Shahaji was very embarrassed with Shivba's behaviour and immediately sent both Jijabai and him back to Poona to avoid further controversy. 'Go home and think over what you have done. Learn to respect our masters. Else you will repent in the future,' Shahaji warned him.

Shivba kept his head bowed and did not say a word. He hadn't meant to disrespect his father. He was simply objecting to the act of bowing down in obeisance like that. People should bow down only in front of God and a king who had earned their respect, Shivba believed. Dadaji Konddev heard about this incident from other officers on the estate. He broached the subject in Shivba's next class.

'Shivba, why did you refuse to bow in front of Adil Shah? It must have appeared very disrespectful to him and embarrassing for your father,' he said.

'I didn't mean to be disrespectful. But why should my father bow down that low for anyone? Just because he is his employer? Don't you say that a good king has to earn his respect?' Shivba asked in return.

'But Adil Shah is our employer. He is the one who has bequeathed this estate and land to your father for caretaking. He deserves our respect. You will also soon join his employment. What will you do then?' asked Dadaji.

'Respect, yes. But not awe or reverence. In any case, I will be my own master. And when I am, I won't expect any of my officers to bow to me like that until I have earned that respect,' corrected Shivba.

Dadaji smiled at Shivba's obstinacy. He realised that the boy would bow to no one—neither Adil Shah nor the Nizam in the south nor the Mughals in the north. From that time on, he started viewing Shivba's courage and adventures in a different light. He started grooming Shivba with the discipline and leadership skills that he would require to be on his own in the future. He mentored his ward in martial exercises, law and order, investigations and disputes, battlefield strategy and civic and administrative matters.

When he was around thirteen or fourteen, Dadaji started delegating a few matters for Shivba to oversee himself and even authorised him to issue orders as his father's representative. Instead of foisting his own disciplinarian nature on Shivba, Dadaji now emphasised on the importance of discipline in maintaining books and law and order in the *jagir*. He highlighted the importance of discipline and justice in the land. Although he continued to refuse to do any reading or writing, Shivba did soak in all the rest of his schooling seriously.

Shivba's supervision and leadership also attracted the youth to him. Several young boys—Mavlas from the Maval region around Poona—became ardent followers and friends. Shivba's first gang of comrades like Yesaji Kank, Baji Pasalkar, Tanaji Malusare came from nearby villages. Dadaji used these young leaders to supervise the borders and important areas in the region to control robberies, thefts and petty crimes.

Soon, these efforts by Dadaji started paying
People felt much safer; military power was co
agriculture gave much better yields and reven
multiplying. Poona became peaceful and prospe
Dadaji's watchful and disciplined eye.

It is said that Dadaji was very strict about c
criminals. Once, the gatekeepers caught a man s
the village and brought them to Dadaji as he wa
something important with Shivba.

'Sir, this man was caught stealing in the villa
the watchman.

'Tie him up in the village chowk for two da
him hungry,' ordered Dadaji. The man was swiftl
Shivba felt bad for the man. He had looked poor.

'Could we not have pardoned the man? He d
a thief. Stealing is definitely wrong but as rulers
should we not think about why people would
asked Shivba as he saw the men taking him awa

'Shivba, just because he doesn't look like a
mean he isn't one. He was caught stealing
caught stealing is pardoned, it sets an examp
that it is okay to steal in this *jagir*. Everyone wil

Leadership Lesson #6

Justice has to be swift and decisive. Jus
delayed is justice denied.

nething or the other. Instead, when you punish one thief public, it discourages the hundreds of thieves who will him every time they pass by the village chowk. A ruler's ength and power are derived most from law and order d the swiftness of justice in his kingdom. Pardoning such act will make you appear weak in front of your people,' plained Dadaji.

Once though, Dadaji's love for justice almost cost him own hand. It is said that Dadaji had a list of punishments different types of crimes in his rulebook for offenders. d often, the punishment was not commensurate to crime committed. Dadaji's punishment for a crime as ple as plucking a fruit from a tree was to cut off the hand he thief. Shivba thought that this punishment was quite eme. According to him, justice also had to be dealt with he right context. A thief stealing food or fruit out of perate need could not be treated in the same manner as ief stealing for monetary gain and greed. But he didn't w how to argue that out with Dadaji until an opportunity sented itself.

Dadaji Konddev had planted a huge garden of trees in the te and named it after Shahaji. He would personally oversee gardening and upkeep of that plot of land. He would also an account of the mangoes, jackfruits and other fruits ving there. Once, he was doing the rounds of the garden with ba and their gardening staff in attendance. As he pulled a ch to inspect a tree, he accidentally plucked a mango. He ed to see Shivba watching him.

'Dadaji, you plucked a mango from your own tree. You committed a crime! Now what will you do?' exclaimed Shivba excitedly.

Dadaji was stoic. He said, 'It is not my tree. It is a tree owned by your father, Shri Shahaji. This is indeed a crime. The law is equal for everyone. I must be given the punishment meant for this crime. My hand should be cut off. Soldier, bring the sword.'

This was his chance, Shivba thought, as he witnessed the unease of onlookers and the gardening staff. 'Soldier, wait! Dadaji, I witnessed you committing the crime and I am aware that you did not intend to pluck the fruit,' he intervened.

'True. But a misdeed is a misdeed. I must be punished for this. It is an order from me,' clarified Dadaji.

'Yes, you should be punished severely. But the order will have to go in my name, isn't it? And so, as the person who issues the ordinance, I am authorised to determine your punishment. Keeping in mind the fact that your transgression was not deliberate, it is actually your hand that committed the crime. It was not your mind that planned it. I declare that from now on, your offending hand should be tied to your chest with a cloth so that it can no longer waver and steal fruits,' declared Shivba with a flourish.

Dadaji smiled. He now understood what his Shivba meant when he said that justice had to be delivered in context. That a ruler who cared about his people should not only punish those who steal but also reflect over why they felt the need to steal. The lad was only a teen but, in him, Dadaji saw the makings of a self-made royal. This man is fit to be a Chhatrapati, he concluded to himself.

Chapter 4

Torna: Shivba's First Adventure

By the time Shivba was in his early teens, it was obvious to everyone around him that he was a born leader. He knew his land like the back of his hand. He wandered over all the steep hills, rivers, fields and forests around. He had acquainted himself with farmers, craftsmen, conmen and soldiers in every nook and corner of the *jagir*. As his knowledge and expertise grew, so did his decisiveness in administrative policy work. The local chiefs started supporting him actively. Slowly, he started acquiring a following among his people for being a fair and just leader. Men would go to him to complain of being conned out of their land holdings or their life's earnings. Women trusted him enough to complain about being molested or harassed by other men or of their husbands abandoning them. Shivba's justice, as his mother had advised, was quick and fitting.

The growing chaos and instability that infighting between the Nizam, Adil Shah and the Mughals had fostered in Maharashtra had been leading to a general sense of hopelessness among the people. There was no leader who truly cared about the people of the region and Shivba had decided that he wanted to do something to regain control of the situation. Choosing a career like his father—that of being employed with and beholden to a king who didn't care about his subjects, except to see them as a source of land revenue—didn't sit right with him.

Shivba was determined that he would lead the Marathas in their quest to find a life of dignity and respect for themselves. He wanted to realise Jijabai's dream of Swarajya—a motherland that the Marathas would call their own—in Maharashtra. But establishing his own rule meant making some very powerful enemies, who had strong and capable armies, fortifications in every region, tremendous military acumen and a full treasury that could fund many battles for many years. Shivba knew he had none of this.

Leadership Lesson #7

At first, try convincing, then try bribing or incentivising. If that doesn't work, try punishment. And when nothing else works, use force.

All he had was a dream and the support of his people. And they were all willing to die to make a difference. So, he decided to focus on that instead.

His charisma and straight talk drew young boys around him who also wanted to make a difference to their society. Most of the strong ones became the henchmen executing his orders—investigating thefts; punishing and locking up outlaws; roughing up men who harassed women; looking for missing children or women; training younger boys in wrestling, horse riding or sword fighting—around the region. There were others who were not so skilled in military action but wanted to be useful nevertheless. Jijabai advised Shivba to recruit them for information.

'Remember the story of the tiny squirrel that Lord Ram recruited to build the legendary bridge, Ram Setu, to reach Ravan's Lanka? She also played a big role in that project; she picked small stones that would fill the gaps between the big ones. Anyone with true honesty and loyalty can be useful to their leader. And intelligence and information about the enemy can sometimes be more crucial in winning a battle than strength of soldiers on the field,' Jijabai reminded him.

So young men who couldn't be recruited in Shivba's gang of soldiers were appointed informally to spy on people and observe goings-on around the villages. Soon enough, there was an extremely efficient and speedy network of information exchange functioning for Shivba.

It is this very informal information system that helped the seventeen-year-old capture his very first fort in 1646. Shivba's informants—sometimes teens hanging around village chowks or travelling traders from Bijapur or Ahmednagar—would often bring news of latest developments to Shivba's ears.

Around this time, there were some talk around the failing health of Adil Shah, the king of Bijapur. Shivba and his crew had started hearing rumours of the king not attending court or being present during important meetings. Apparently, his wife, Badi Sahiba, was the one issuing most of the orders. Although the king's military campaigns were on track, they also heard of *hakims* and medicine men frequenting the king's bedchambers.

Through their team of informants, they had also heard that the officer in charge of the Torna fort was incompetent. The fort was a huge, sprawling structure standing atop the Western Ghats on the outskirts of Poona district. It was the tallest fort in that region and was a good vantage point over the whole expanse. It was so large that it was called Prachandagadh (literally meaning large fort). Besides, Shivba was aware that the fort held a lot of Bijapuri treasure. It would be a strategic conquest to win the fort and use the treasure to fund their future campaigns against other Bijapuri land. Dadaji was unwell at the time but Shivba knew that he would not be in favour of such an act of aggression against Bijapur.

Leadership Lesson #8

Focus on your advantages and strengths rather than your disadvantages. Work to your advantages.

He took the idea to Jijabai.

'What if I took some troops and attacked Torna? The man in charge of the fort is not very efficient. We can quickly overpower him,' suggested Shivba.

Jijabai thought about this for a few moments and then reacted.

'Shivba, your force is very small compared to his. Besides, once Adil Shah hears about your attack, he will be provoked into a counter attack, which may prove to be expensive for our side. Perhaps, a quieter approach is required. Make sure you always use the strategy of *saam, daam, dand* and *bhed* when getting your work done. At first, try convincing; then try bribing or incentivising, then try punishment. Only when none of the first three approaches work, try war,' warned Jijabai.

'True,' Shivba agreed. 'We have a small gang and a big fight with their well-equipped force would prove to be much worse for us,' he said. Shivba decided that it would be better if they did this quietly and swiftly so as to take their enemy completely by surprise.

That is how he conceptualised the innovative strategy of *ganimikawa*—what we now know as guerilla warfare—the art of attacking sneakily but swiftly in small groups so as to create shock and awe to overpower a larger army.

Shivba and his crew decided that they would take advantage of the fort's altitude and the mountain and dense vegetation surrounding it. They decided that three of Shivba's crew—Baji Pasalkar, Yesaji Kank and Tanaji Malusare—would take a group of Mavlas each and hide in the vegetation around the fort in the evening. Fully aware that the commandant of the fort was lax in his security measures, this small group would spring a sudden attack in the morning and quickly take control of the fort and its treasury before the troops could retaliate. By the time the headquarters in Bijapur heard about the attack, Shivba's team would already have taken control of the treasury and the security around the fort.

The plan was successful and, within no time, Shivba and his group of Mavlas had captured the fort. The group also discovered treasure worth two lakh *hun* (currency of the day in Bijapur).

The capture of Torna is said to be a momentous first step in Shivaji Maharaj's quest for Swarajya. He also started preparing for when the news would reach Bijapur and how Adil Shah would react.

But as Jijabai had suggested, all wars need not be fought on the battlefield. Some problems can be fixed with the right communication through the right channels. It was time to use the second step of incentivising people to get work done. Shivba sent a few informants to Bijapur to bribe the ministers in Adil Shah's court. These ministers recreated a favourable narrative which highlighted the neglected state of Torna and

Leadership Lesson #9

All wars need not be fought on the battlefield. Some problems can be fixed with the right communication through the right channels.

how the brave Shivaji had thrown out the lazy commander-in-charge and his team to take control of the administrative affairs there. Shahaji, who was until then unaware of Shivba's actions and motivations, is also said to have supported this story and temporarily allayed the king's suspicions.

Blessed with this reprieve and the Torna treasure that would help him recruit more soldiers and better ammunition, Shivba started planning what his next steps towards Swarajya would be. Around this period, Dadaji Konddev's health took a turn for the worse and he passed away. Shivba knew that without Dadaji's watchful eye and supervision, Shahaji's *jagir* around Pune would be in peril.

Dadaji had always said, 'The manner and discipline with which a kingdom is governed shows the strength of the king ruling it.' So Shivba decided to bring the whole region and its forts under his own administrative control immediately. It was in the aftermath of annexing the Torna fort that Shivba and his first crew-cum-companions took the oath of Swarajya in the temple of the deity, Rayreshwar.

'This, the capture of Torna, is but the first step towards our dream of Swarajya. We shall aim to attain Swarajya, our own kingdom, meant to take care of our own people. It will be a

Leadership Lesson #10

Every small contribution helps in a big goal.
Use every resource you have.

kingdom that belongs to its people and not its Rajah. We shall work hard to make the dream come true,' they all swore.

Shivaji started allocating formal roles and responsibilities to his troop of soldiers basis their skills and abilities. He hired a chief minister, a *peshwa*, an accountant, a secretary, a couple of paymasters for the soldiers and a commander-in-chief. He offered his soldiers a steady salary because most of them were agriculturists whose families would suffer and starve when they were out fighting for their motherland. Fixing a salary for his soldiers meant that their families would be supported by a stable income. This also reduced corruption and looting by royal troops which was common in those days.

He quickly ordered the construction of another fort, Rajgarh, around Torna with more fortifications (*machi*) on all sides. He set up outposts on all important borders and started planning which Bijapuri *jagirs* they could annex next.

Interestingly, it was this *ganimikawa* strategy and manipulation, rather than bravery in battlefare, that came in handy during the next few acquisitions Shivba made. Let's see how.

Chapter 5

Saam-Daam-Dand-Bhed: How to Be a King

Capturing Torna the way he did was a bold act of aggression. Shivba wanted to make his next moves quickly but by winning over the local *jagirdaars* on the Bijapuri payroll to his side rather than antagonising them. This proved to be rather difficult. This is where Jijabai's mantra of '*Saam-daam-dand-bhed*' proved to be really effective for Shivba.

It so happened that one of the *jagirs* in Supa, near Ahmednagar, had been handed over to Shambhuji Mohite, the brother of Shahaji's second wife, Tukabai. On Dadaji's passing, he refused to take orders from Shivaji and demanded that Shahaji hand over the administration of the *jagir* to him directly. Shivba was in a fix. He did not want to antagonise a relative but he did not want to pardon disobedience either.

Like Dadaji used to say, 'Pardoning such disobedience makes a leader appear weak in front of his people.' Jijabai also warned, 'Shivba you need to make an example of Shambhuji. Else, it will be difficult for you to persuade other *jagirdaars* to support you. They seek strength in their leader.'

It was time to use *dand* or punishment as a strategy.

So, Shivba devised a ploy. He had learned from his spies that Shambhuji was leaving for a holiday. He sent some Mavlas to capture and imprison Shambhuji when he was on his way. Shivba then went with some troops and officers and attacked Shambhuji's properties. During imprisonment, when Shambhuji continued to refuse to obey Shivba, he was sent off packing directly to Shahaji with little else than a few belongings.

This ploy offered a dual advantage to Shivba. First, Supa was brought under Shivba's control. Second, other *jagirdaars* who were hesitant to lend Shivba support, quickly capitulated. The fort of Chakan and other adjoining regions were also quickly acquired by *saam*—negotiations and convincing. When Shivba learnt from his informants that the Bijapuri commander of the Kondana fort was corrupt, he didn't waste any time in sending a bribe and took control of that fort too. Here, he used *daam*—bribery—as a means of getting what he wanted.

Leadership Lesson #11

Know your enemy. Befriend the enemies of your enemy.

With all these territories under his control, Shivba started eyeing the fort of Purandar. This Bijapuri fort wasn't an easy acquisition. It was controlled by Nilu Nayak, a greedy man who had inherited the land and its resources from his ancestors. It is said that Nilu was so greedy that he had even cut out his younger brothers from their share of their ancestral land. Shivba's chiefs met with Nilu's brothers to assure them that Shivba could restore their rights over their ancestral estate if they supported him in defeating Nilu. The two brothers agreed to help Shivba.

One evening, during a village celebration, Nilu was captured by his brothers while Shivba's soldiers took possession of the Purandar fort. Shivba immediately sacked Nilu Nayak's staff at the fort and replaced them with his trusted soldiers. The two brothers were given back rights to their ancestral land and compensated generously with other land assets as well.

After Purandar, Rajgarh, Kondana and Torna, followed Rohira, Tikona, Lohgadh and Rajmachi, which brought Shivba closer to Konkan on the west. As Adil Shah's health continued to worsen, Shivba became more and more confident. Shivba followed the policy of 'strike first, strike hard' during the initial stages.

Aware that the wealthy towns of Kalyan and Bhiwandi were not protected by any walls around them, Shivba's men attacked and looted them. Some local *jagirdaars* around this region, tired of their Muslim rulers, even wrote to Shivba of their desire to support his campaign against Bijapur. Shivba quickly added these to his roster and ordered another couple of forts to be built as well.

It was his eventual conquest of the Raigarh fort and its political consequences that proved to be the biggest challenge for young Shivba.

The Bijapur court finally took cognisance of the news of his successes and consolidation. Adil Shah's advisers recommended that action be taken against him. However, they did not directly confront Shivba himself. The Bijapur court ordered the arrest of Shahaji and confiscation of all his properties and soldiers. Adil Shah sent his very formidable general, Afzal Khan, to make the arrest.

Shivba had not foreseen this. His father had always been a Bijapuri loyalist. While he was not particularly close to Shahaji, Shivba had never imagined that his bold and ambitious attacks would impact his father's career. It is said that the law enforcers in Bijapur kept Shahaji in a cell and continued building a slow wall around him every day to pressurise him to summon Shivba to Bijapur to surrender.

Shivba was in a dilemma. He did not want to surrender to Adil Shah and appear weak to his Maratha people. Neither did he want to relinquish his father to Adil Shah's mercies. Besides, he knew that his father's arrest and hardships would unduly worry his mother.

Leadership Lesson #12

Diplomacy can prove less costly than war.

'*Aaisaheb*, what should I do? This is an impossible situation. I don't want to sacrifice everything my men have achieved by capitulating to the enemy. But *Babasaheb* will be punished if I don't surrender,' a worried Shivba vocalised to his mother.

'Shivba, don't be afraid. A king often has to go through such difficult phases. Acquiring power is easy but holding on to it is not. Diplomacy is an important aspect of politics. The solution is not in battle but in diplomatic negotiations. Adil Shah is not afraid of the Marathas, so he will not be amenable to negotiating your father's release with us. We need to think of someone stronger than Adil Shah who can intervene on our behalf and pressurise him to release your father,' suggested Jijabai.

Given the geopolitical situation around, Shivba could only think of one ally who was in a position to help. The Mughal empire was constantly vying to establish itself more firmly in the Deccan region against the Bijapur Sultanate. It was also powerful enough to intimidate Adil Shah. Shivba thus concluded that the enemy of his enemy had to be befriended.

'We must ally with the Mughal empire. That is the only way,' Shivba declared to his ministers.

The earliest powada, inspirational poem, is supposed to be *The Killing of Afzal Khan* by poet and performer Agnidas. Other legendary powadas were written and performed by Maharashtrian shahirs (poets) on other heroes like Tanaji Malusare and Baji Pasalkar in Shivaji Maharaj's army. The powadas have been a rich source of oral history of Maharashtra.

'But why will the Mughal Emperor agree to do this for us?' they asked with surprise.

'Because we will help him consolidate his strength and power in the Deccan and Maharashtra against Bijapur,' claimed Shivba.

So, Shivba's minister wrote to the Mughal viceroy in Deccan requesting him to put in a word to Adil Shah for Shahaji's release in return for Shivba's service in favour of the Mughal forces. Although the Mughal court did acknowledge the offer, the emperor did not take a definite stance.

When that move did not work, Shivba enlisted the help of two other Muslim nobles and former colleagues of Shahaji in Adil Shah's employ to broker peace on his behalf with the assurance that Shivba would no longer be a threat to the king.

After a few months of deliberation, Adil Shah released Shahaji on the condition that he would not make any mischief or aid his son in any of his activities. The truce was, however, very short-lived. It was suspended soon after the news of the killing of Shivba's elder brother, Sambhaji, in battle, on behalf of Bijapur in Karnataka.

This series of episodes taught young Shivba a very important lesson. Every battle has its consequences. It was

Leadership Lesson #13

Timing is everything. Bide your time well; wait for the right opportunity.

not enough to just be strong and brave in battle. He had very powerful enemies in all directions. Diplomacy, tact and alliances were important as well. And that there was a time and place for everything.

Just after Shahaji's release, Bijapur did make an attempt to capture Shivba. A Maratha warrior and his team was ordered to find out where Shivba was and to capture and bring him to Adil Shah's court. Fortunately, the captors had the wrong intel and reached Mahad, near Raigarh in North Konkan, while Shivba was busy with administrative work in some other city. He heard about the attempt and escaped to one of his forts while his soldiers sneak-attacked the captors and sent them packing. This act from Bijapur was indeed a provocation designed for Shivba to retaliate in some manner.

But the otherwise impatient Shivba was wiser. He realised that his focus was required in consolidating his newly-acquired land and enforcing the right laws and administration in those regions. There would be a time and place to avenge these acts and he would take action at the right time. Fortunately for Shivba, there did come a right time even though it was four to five years later.

Chapter 6

The Killing of the Great Afzal Khan

Shivba bided his time for the next few years after his father's release. He focussed his efforts on the smooth running of the land and forts he had annexed. He also especially maintained good relations with the Mughal forces. He was happy to wait for the Mughals to decimate Bijapur and Ahmednagar. Prince Aurangzeb had just started his campaign against the Qutub Shahi rulers in Golconda and Adil Shah's health kept deteriorating further. There was absolutely no point in antagonising such a powerful enemy at that particular point of time. In fact, Shivba was quite conciliatory in his correspondence to Aurangzeb and the Mughal regime in the mid-1650s. Prince Aurangzeb had been informed of Shivba's cunning and diplomacy. He had been regularly updated on Shivba's daring stunts and guerilla tactics, making him a threat to be taken seriously. But since Shivba's attention was on Adil Shah losing hold over his territory, he was prepared to wait and watch how far things went.

During this time, Shivba and his soldiers were busy raiding parts of Ahmednagar district and carrying off cash, horses and jewellery which resulted in a few heavy skirmishes with the Mughal forces supporting Ahmed Shah. Although Aurangzeb's men managed to stall Shivba's soldiers, much of the harm was already done.

These skirmishes made Aurangzeb aware of Shivba's deceptive strengths and the unpredictability of the geographic region of Maharashtra, as well. He knew that Shivba's troops were the experts in those hills and forests.

That is why when the prince eventually started peace talks with the ailing Adil Shah, he asked him to categorically tackle Shivba's menace once and for all, so that it would not become a threat to the Mughal empire. He also spent a lot of money to repair Bijapuri forts outside Poona, so as to keep a watch on Shivba's activities.

Adil Shah's forces decided to finally 'solve' the Shivba problem. But open battle was not an option. After the enormous losses of their battle against the Mughals, the Bijapuri forces were in no state to launch an offensive on Shivba's troops. Besides, it would be difficult to defeat the Maratha warrior on his own turf—the steep hills and forests of the Western Ghats.

It was therefore decided that a subtle approach would be preferable. The ministers went to the warrior, the great Afzal Khan. As a general, he was equal to the best warriors in Bijapur. He was known not only for his brute strength but also his courage and fearlessness. He also had a sizeable force reporting to him.

'Great sir, at the behest of our Queen Badi Sahiba, we have a highly important mission for you—the capture of Shivaji,' requested the head of the council of ministers in Bijapur.

'The brave Maratha warrior? I have a sizeable force. It would be an honour to defeat him for our country, Your Honour,' acquiesced Afzal Khan.

'Sir, you do not have to fight him. We need to capture or, if need be, murder him, as per the Queen's instructions,' corrected the minister.

'But why will Shivaji meet me of all people? Surely, he will be suspicious as to why a Bijapuri warrior wants to meet him?' asked a puzzled Afzal Khan.

'You could pretend to make an offer of peace to him. Accordingly, we will send diplomatic officers to approach him to negotiate peace terms and set up a meeting with you,' suggested the minister.

'If we were to fight in open battle, I could capture Shivaji without even getting off my horse. But a diplomatic

Leadership Lesson #14
A good leader always relies on the good sense and intelligence of their troops and only takes a decision in favour of the well-being of all their people.

negotiation is tricky. Let me plan this campaign in my way,' confessed Afzal Khan.

The general strategised on what his next steps would be. Shivba could be treated with some of his own medicine: hitting fast and hard. But he also knew that to get Shivba to meet him, he would need diplomatic efforts. And without Shivba's capture, Afzal Khan's mission would be incomplete.

Shock and awe at first, and then a hand of peace, that's how he would proceed, Afzal Khan decided. Without wasting any time and before spies could convey the information, Afzal Khan started proceeding toward Poona. Along the way, he ordered his soldiers to destroy idols in many temples in Shivba's territory, the most important of all being the idol of Bhavani Mata, the family deity of the Bhonsles. He knew that this outrageous crime would enrage Shivaji, who was proud of his culture, faith and his people. In a fit of rage, Shivaji was likely to make a mistake and come and confront him.

He also bribed a few local chiefs with money and the promise of lucrative positions to help him lure Shivba out of his fortress and capture him. Around the same time, another missive was sent directly to Shivba with an offer for peace and a discussion involving him being given a powerful position as a noble in the Bijapur court. These combined actions did manage to spook Shivba's men. They didn't understand which information to trust.

'*Raje*, the great Afzal Khan has desecrated the idol of our patron goddess, *Ma* Tulja Bhavani,' said one informant who came from near Tuljapur.

'*Raje*, the great Afzal Khan has sent an officer with a request to meet you. He was a great friend of your father, Shahaji *Raje*. He wants to formalise your ownership of the forts annexed from them and broker peace with you on behalf of Bijapur. He also wants to discuss a position for you in the Bijapuri court,' said another informant.

Shivba was perplexed. On the one hand, he was enraged at the blasphemy committed against his faith by the destruction of idols. He wanted to go and confront Afzal Khan's troops immediately. But, on the other hand, he was aware that those actions could only have some ulterior motive, the purpose of which was not clear to him yet.

Like a good leader, Shivba did not react hastily. He called a meeting of his local chiefs and administrators.

'Shivba, it is better to understand the pros and cons of every action before you commit to it. A good leader always relies on the good sense and intelligence of his troops and only takes a decision in favour of the well-being of all his men,' Jijabai often advised.

Shivba did an audit of his forces, cavalry and ammunition. He also reviewed all the information his men had brought on Afzal Khan and the general's troops and weaponry. Some men brought updated news on Afzal Khan's aggressive actions throughout Maharashtra.

Khan had come with a lot of men and it looked like he was prepared to stay till his objective, whatever it was, was met. Afzal Khan also looked like he was intent on creating trouble. The legend of Afzal Khan and his military actions had also intimidated

Shivba's men a bit. So far, they were used to small and quick battles planned to precision. They weren't sure of how things would work out if the battle prolonged beyond a few days.

'*Raje*, we have built our ammunitions and trained our men. But so far, they are not used to prolonged attacks. We are also not suited to play defensive. Afzal Khan's actions indicate that he will attack in a moment, given the right provocation. All of us would willingly give up our lives for you and our motherland. But confronting Afzal Khan at the moment would not be a wise course of action,' suggested his chief minister.

Shivba took in the opinions of his men. He believed in their judgement. 'A leader is only as good as his men. Confronting Afzal Khan would not be a good move. But then, I am not sure what he aims to achieve with this meeting either,' confessed Shivba.

'Yes sir. He is a cunning man. Refusing to meet him would also antagonise him and the Bijapur court,' agreed his ministers.

'Let us think of a way to conduct this meeting in the most diplomatic manner possible. It is most advisable to play to our strengths. Perhaps you should take the time to think this over,' suggested Jijabai.

Leadership Lesson #15

Believe the best of people's intentions but always assume the worst and be prepared for it.

That night, Shivba went to sleep with worries, insecurities and battle strategies running in his head. The next step was critical for the future of his motherland and Shivba himself. If the meeting was successful, he would be one step closer to his dream of Hindavi Swaraj. But if he was captured or had to capitulate for any reason, he would forever have to live with this defeat.

It is said young Shivba had a vision that night. He dreamt of Goddess Tulja Bhavani.

'Shivba, do not forgive those who disrespect the religion and gods of others. Do not be afraid. Go ahead and face your enemies bravely. You will always have my support. You will never fail as long as you are on the path of the righteous. *Vijayi bhava*,' blessed Goddess Bhavani.

The next morning, Shivba woke up with a new resolve. He decided that an enemy who adopted a sneaky dual strategy of threat as well as reconciliation deserved to be treated in the same manner.

'When one is unsure of the enemy's motivations, one should always assume the worst. We are not born to keep second-guessing ourselves. Let us meet the great Afzal Khan with the best intentions. But let us also be prepared to fight a battle with him if that's what he actually wants,' declared Shivba.

His ministers sent off an envoy of their own to Afzal Khan's envoy to communicate that their chief was willing to meet him as long as he was assured of his personal safety. At the same time, Shivba despatched two sets of troops to proceed quietly towards Pratapgarh and track the goings-on locally.

The Maratha envoy conveyed the message that Shivba was willing to meet Afzal Khan with the best of intentions and an assurance of Afzal Khan's personal safety as well. But the messenger had also been advised to check out where the meeting was to take place and other logistics. It had been proposed that the duo meet at Wai. On his return to Pratapgarh, the messenger conveyed that he thought the meeting place wasn't too safe if Afzal's men decided to go back on their word.

The messenger warned, '*Raje*, the enemy is extremely cunning. We should not trust them. I would recommend that we invite Afzal Khan to a place closer to our fort and that we plan the logistics ourselves so that there is no foul play. We should be prepared thoroughly in case there is.'

Shivba agreed and sent a message to the enemy camp accordingly, with the promise that Afzal Khan would be allowed to return safely after the meeting. Afzal Khan, pleased that Shivba was scared to meet him, graciously agreed. The long road between Wai and Pratapgarh was cleared up to make space for Afzal Khan's troops. Arrangements were made for them to eat and rest at the foothills of the fort.

Afzal Khan's soldiers checked out the meeting place and the *shamiana* that was set up to receive the 'eminent' guest. There were wonderful carpets and comfortable seating. It was a safe point overlooking the valley. Afzal's men were reassured and sanctioned the meeting for the next day. What they did not know was that in his true *ganimikawa* (guerilla) style, Shivba had posted groups of his soldiers all around in the wilderness surrounding the path that led to this meeting place.

It had been decided that both chiefs would arrive with ten men each for security. It had also been decided that neither of the men would carry any weapons in good faith and retain just one bodyguard outside the meeting room for personal security. Just before his meeting, Shivba went to seek his mother's blessings.

'Shivba, be prepared. The man you are going to meet arrested your father. And it is rumoured that he has played some mischief in the death of your elder brother. He is known to be cunning. Be very careful. *Vijayi bhava*,' blessed Jijabai.

Shivba bowed while smiling to himself. He was not going to go out without a fight. For starters, he was aware that Afzal Khan was built huge—he was tall and hefty—while Shivba was of moderate height and build. He would never win against Afzal Khan in a one-on-one wrestle. Shivba had worn a steel cap under his shiny turban to protect his head and an armour under his kurta. Indeed, he was not carrying any weapon in his hands as promised. But he had donned the *waaghnakh* or tiger's claw, a small sharp weapon worn on the fingers and concealed inside his left palm. Under the sleeve of the kurta of his right hand, he had hidden a *bichhwa,* a small sharp dagger. The man with him, Jiva Mahale, was brave, nimble and extremely trustworthy.

During his coronation ceremony, Shivaji Maharaj wore a scarlet robe embroidered with real gold and a silk turban studded with precious pearls. He was weighed separately on a weighing scale with seven metals–gold, silver, copper, zinc, tin, iron, lead–and items such as camphor, butter and sugar. These items, worth Shivaji's weight, were given away to charity.

Afzal Khan arrived first on a grand *palkhi*. The bearers of the *palkhi* and the general's bodyguard, Sayyed Banda were made to wait outside while Afzal Khan was in the *shamiana*. Then Shivba arrived and entered the pavilion. His bodyguard, Jiva Mahale, stood outside.

At the outset, Shivba realised that despite their agreement, Afzal Khan carried a sword by his side. But Shivba did not react to that. It did not hurt for Afzal Khan to believe that Shivba was unarmed and had come to surrender to this great Bijapuri warrior. He bowed respectfully in front of Afzal Khan.

'No, no, *Raje*, friendly agreements should always start with an embrace,' reassured Afzal Khan as he got up. Shivba was the shorter of the two, so Afzal Khan's arms came around his neck and shoulders. It is said that after just a second, Afzal shifted his embrace to tighten his arm around Shivba's neck and drew a dagger to his back. Shivba's body armour thwarted his move. However, in the same instant as he felt himself being strangled, the agile Shivba unclenched his palm and tore open Afzal Khan's stomach with his *waaghnakh*. Just as Afzal's hold loosened, Shivba slid the dagger from under his sleeve, attacked Afzal Khan with the *bichhwa* on his right side and ran swiftly outside the meeting

Leadership Lesson #16

Size doesn't determine success or strength.

room. Seeing Shivba run, Afzal Khan screamed, 'Catch him. Catch him. He is running away.'

Even before the other attendants outside could gather their wits, Shivba had rushed out. Jiva Mahale jumped up instantly and started running behind him. Just then Afzal Khan's bodyguard Sayyad Banda raised his sword to swing it hard at Shivba. In the nick of time, Jiva stepped in to fend off the attack and swiftly killed Sayyad Banda.

By this time, Afzal Khan's attendants had rushed to him and were picking him up to carry him to safety. But another of Shivba's attendants directly attacked the bearers of the *palkhi* and then the injured Afzal Khan, beheading him.

Another attendant rushed to the top of Pratapgarh and fired a cannon. This was the signal that Shivba's guerilla troops were waiting for. They immediately jumped out of hiding and headed to attack the Bijapuri troops at the foothills who were totally caught unaware and started fleeing in panic. Shivba's troops took advantage of this and went on a rampage further downhill to where the rest of the Bijapuri troops were camped. Very little was spared while all the ammunition, treasure, money, tents, belongings, horses, elephants and camels were taken away. Some men and women were taken prisoners as was the practice after battle in those days.

That night, Shivba's soldiers rejoiced. This was their first taste of real victory against a powerful enemy. They had managed to imprison a lot of senior Bijapuri soldiers, including Afzal Khan's son.

'Be graceful in victory as well as defeat, Shivba,' suggested Jijabai when she blessed Shivba on his return.

The very next day, an appraisal of the prisoners and the loot was carried out. Remembering his mother's words, Shivba first respectfully let go of the captured women and children who had been brought to their camp after the battle. He then paid and let go of some of the brave soldiers from the enemy camp as well. With the loot, Shivba rewarded his own soldiers. He generously rewarded the sons of those of his soldiers who died during battle with jobs and widows with money. Those who were injured were given money and jewellery.

This episode captured the imagination of Shivba's people all over Maharashtra and Karnataka. *Powadas* have been written and performed, inspired by Shivaji's bravery. Over the centuries, the legend of Afzal Khan's killing has been visualised as the glorious avenging of good over evil. This was the first step towards the Swarajya that Jijabai and her son had envisioned.

Chapter 7

The Battle of Pawankhind

The news of Shivaji's victory over Afzal Khan spread like wildfire. Needless to say, it not only embarrassed Bijapur but also alerted the Mughals in the north. Aurangzeb finally realised that he could no longer underestimate the Maratha chief. He also realised that the Bijapur forces were not as strong as they seemed to be.

He posted his uncle, the brave Shaista Khan, to head the Deccan campaign and to keep a close eye on Shivaji. He was also supportive of the Bijapur administration tackling the Shivba menace. Because of this tacit understanding between his two foes, Shivaji's forces had to fight on two fronts and got thwarted in many battles.

When Shivba conquered Panhala, a fort near Kolhapur, from the hands of the Bijapuri forces, Ali Adil Shah, the new heir to Bijapur, felt that Shivaji needed to be stopped in his tracks. He made a deal with Siddi Jauhar, an Abyssinian slave-general and ruler of Kurnool, to go and attack Shivaji with the help of the Bijapuri army. On the other hand, the Mughals had already attacked Poona and wrested it out of Shivaji's control.

Jauhar proceeded with his army to Panhala where Shivaji was living at the moment. Jauhar was aware that much of Shivaji's force was in Poona, dealing with the Mughals. He decided he would pressure Shivaji into battle with him. Jauhar, along with Afzal Khan's son, Fazal Khan, reached Panhalgadh and lay siege to the fort.

He asked his forces to surround the fort from all sides so that not a single person could enter or leave it without getting caught. Shivaji's chief of forces, Netaji Palkar, rushed to Panhala but was defeated and sent back. Over the next few days, Siddi Jauhar's men built small lookout structures along the boundaries and installed sophisticated Mughal canons and artillery that would shoot right inside the fort. He was hoping to flush out the Maratha chief once and for all.

The siege went on for weeks. Besides, the Mughal forces were running amok in and around Poona. Sources reported that they were eyeing the Chakan fort. They needed to be contained and sent back.

Leadership Lesson #17

Even in escape or surrender, be strategic so as to lose the least.

Shivba was trapped inside his own fort and Siddi Jauhar's men had gone on the offensive. It had been a long time since the enemy had allowed any food or fresh supplies to be delivered inside the fort. Shivba was getting desperate. He had to get out but he didn't know what to do. He had frequent meetings with the sardars who were inside the fort with him.

'*Raje*, Siddi Jauhar looks like he is prepared to wait for a lifetime. Protecting the fort is becoming impossible day by day. It is imperative that we get you and your family out of here safely. Saving your life is of the utmost importance because that is the only way Swarajya can survive,' advised Shivba's trusted chief, Baji Prabhu Deshpande.

'I agree. But this escape is not without risk. We have only five-hundred soldiers while they have thousands of troops. Besides, if this escape is foiled, we will all be summarily killed. But if we don't escape this dangerous trap, we will be killed, anyway. Losing the fort is not the issue. When we escape, it has to be done strategically so as to incur the least loss of lives of our soldiers. Remember, we can fight our next fight but only if we survive now,' warned Jijabai.

Shivaji considered both opinions. He remembered one of his younger soldiers saying that there was a wild hidden path out of the Panhala fort.

'Perhaps we could sneak out of the fort through that wild forest path and rush to Vishalgarh with our soldiers,' commented Shivaji.

'You are right, *Raje*. But there is a logistical issue with that idea,' warned Baji Prabhu. 'The moment Siddi's troops realise that you have escaped, they will follow suit. They are not so familiar with our territory but they have a lot of troops. Ghodkhind is an extremely narrow pass—only one horse can pass through it at a time. And it is the only access point to reach Vishalgarh. With so many of us, this pass will not be easy to navigate with someone at our heels,' he said.

'It would make sense then to keep Siddi Jauhar unaware of our escape for as long as we can. We will need to somehow reassure him that everything is normal with the siege. This way, we will have a head start in our journey to Vishalgarh,' recommended Shivaji.

'Yes, *Raje*. And at the entry of Ghodkhind, I will wait with our soldiers and hold fort, restricting Siddi's men from following you up to Vishalgarh,' suggested Baji Prabhu. He went on to assemble the Mavlas who were expert navigators in the dense forests of Panhala.

So, it was decided to first allay Siddi Jauhar's suspicions by reassuring him that everything was going according to his plan. Panhala had been under siege for around four months by then. Shivaji sent a messenger to Siddi Jauhar with the message that he was ready to surrender and relinquish the fort. The messenger also conveyed Shivaji's earnest request

Leadership Lesson #18

When stuck in difficult circumstances, take the time to understand the lay of the land and imminent threats.

to meet with him soon to formalise the terms of the Maratha chief's defeat and retirement. Siddi Jauhar readily agreed, relieved that the siege was about to end soon. It hadn't been easy on his troops either.

Shivaji came with his trusted soldiers to meet Siddi Jauhar at midnight. They discussed the terms of his surrender and assurance of his safety. Knowing Siddi Jauhar's ambitions, Shivaji also assured him of support towards a larger campaign to form his very own kingdom in the future. They both took an oath solemnising this promise. Siddi Jauhar gifted Shivaji a brightly coloured gemstone-studded turban. Shivaji wore the turban and went back.

The next night was a full moon night. Shivaji prepared to escape. He and his family dressed as simple soldiers and left Panhala with less than a hundred men alongside them. As decided, Baji Prabhu was to trail them till the narrow pass of Ghodkhind and thwart Siddi's men in order to buy time so that Shivaji could reach Vishalgarh and fire the cannons from the top of the fort.

'Baji Prabhu, this is not an easy task. Siddi Jauhar has around ten thousand men and you will have only three hundred. Come what may, you will have to hold fort,' warned Jijabai with concern when he came to seek her blessings before leaving.

Baji Prabhu stood tall with pride. 'If I have to even give up my life for *Raje* and my motherland, there is no bigger achievement. Please bless me so I can do my duty,' he said sincerely. He touched Jijabai's feet and left to follow Shivaji, protecting his group from the rear end. The group was to sneak out by the secret forest path to Vishalgarh. The full moon night was chosen for better visibility.

By the evening, Siddi's men had heard about the truce between their leaders and were relieved that the siege would end without a battle. There was an air of relaxation around Panhalgadh. The enemy was looking forward to going home soon. As they relaxed and chatted around the fire along the border of the fort at midnight, they saw a group of men on horses. Among them was Shivaji, wearing the bright turban that Siddi Jauhar had gifted him. Some soldiers rushed to get their horses ready while some hurried to alert Jauhar. Jauhar, his son Siddi Masood and Fazal Khan immediately followed suit. The path was rough and the group took long to catch up with the group of fleeing Marathas. However, once overtaken, Siddi Jauhar realised they had been conned. The man who was wearing the colourful turban was not Shivaji at all! He was a lookalike.

This had been the plan of the Marathas all along. Shivba must have escaped already, Siddi Jauhar realised in alarm. He led his troops in the direction of the wild forest path that he suspected Shivaji to have taken. Hot on his heels rushed Siddi Masood and Fazal Khan with the rest of their troops.

Leadership Lesson #19
Distract, then attack.

As the troops accompanying the real Shivaji reached Ghodkhind, they started passing it one by one while Baji Prabhu set up his troop formation to hide around, awaiting the arrival of the Bijapuri forces. They arrived soon enough and were shocked, yet again, to find Maratha men attacking them from all sides. Baji Prabhu attacked the enemy fiercely. But there were too many of them and he realised that victory was impossible.

'Saving *Raje*'s life is of utmost importance because that is the only way to Swarajya. I will have to keep fighting and thwarting the enemy till I hear the sound of the cannons,' he thought to himself.

Baji Prabhu Deshpande fought valiantly against the Bijapuri forces. Even when on the verge of defeat, his army of Bandal, a sub-community of Maratha warriors, fought with all their strength and passion. Although they were badly injured, beaten up, trampled upon, cut to pieces and as good as dead, they didn't collapse or dare stop breathing. Till his last breath, Baji Prabhu kept fighting. It was only when he finally heard the loud firing of cannons from atop Vishalgarh, signalling that Shivaji had safely reached, that he allowed himself to give up his life with a quiet sigh of 'Har Har Mahadev'.

Shivaji's army had to fight Bijapuri forces at Vishalgarh as well. But they were quickly defeated because Shivba's

Shivaji built many naval forts in his time. Many historians consider him the first king who developed a naval force by constructing prominent forts around the big ports along the Konkan coast.

troops had caught them completely by surprise. When Shivba thought of Baji Prabhu Deshpande's bravery and sacrifice, it brought tears of gratitude to his eyes. He summoned Baji Prabhu's young son and offered him employment within his army and rewarded his family with land. 'The narrow pass of Ghodkhind has been purified by the blood of my soldiers and the sacrifice of their lives. This place will hereon be called Pawankhind,' he declared with pride.

The battle of Pawankhind proved to be the last major battle between Shivaji Maharaj and Bijapur. Although Panhala was taken by Bijapuri forces, the embarrassment of Shivaji's escape right from under Siddi Jauhar's eyes proved too much for him. He didn't pursue the annexation of Vishalgarh and retreated to his own territory soon.

Chapter 8

The Cutting of Shaista Khan's Fingers

While Shivaji had been busy dealing with Siddi Jauhar in Panhala, Shaista Khan proceeded to annex many Maratha strongholds and forts around Poona. A little before the siege of Panhala, Shaista Khan had been wreaking havoc in Poona and had captured Shivaji's estate and childhood home for himself. Shivba's men gave a valiant defence, even to the extent of blocking the Mughal army's access to grains and fodder and other provisions. But they stood no chance against the Mughal chief and his troops.

Shaista Khan was also working to a brief: to hunt down Shivaji and put him out of action. Emperor Aurangzeb warned Shaista Khan before he left for his campaign in Maharashtra.

'Plan your strategy well. He is a mountain rat (*pahadon ka chooha*). Do not underestimate him,' warned the emperor.

'Do not worry *Jahanpanaah*. I know how to deal with mountain rats,' assured Shaista Khan.

After Purandar and some smaller forts, Shaista Khan had been busy with the acquisition of the Chakan fort. The Maratha troops were led by the brave Firangji Narsala, who was an old-time Shivaji loyalist. He had been informed that Shivaji was busy dealing with the Bijapuri forces at Panhala and could not spare any army to come to his help at Chakan. He had been briefed to fight with all his might but surrender in case of an emergency. The Mughal army was not used to heavy rains that lashed this part of Maharashtra and Shivaji's troops took full advantage of the weather to give a tough fight to the enemy. The siege of the Chakan fort went on for more than two months, it is said.

Firangji's men took more than three-hundred lives and wounded more than six-hundred men. It is said that Shaista Khan was so impressed with Firangji Narsala's leadership and military acumen that he offered him a position in the Mughal army with a high salary. But Firangji refused, declaring his loyalty to Shivaji.

Leadership Lesson #20

Shame and embarrassment can hurt way more than a physical injury.

'If you do not wish to join our forces, it is your choice. But your loyalty towards that mountain rat is misplaced,' laughed Shaista Khan and allowed Firangji Narsala to go back to his master with his army.

Shaista Khan returned to Poona pleased with his victory over the Maratha troops but also alert to the fact that defeating Shivaji and his guerilla Mavla army, that was light on its feet and skilled in navigating the wilderness and slopes of the Western Ghats, was no mean task. It was not going to be as quickly accomplished as Emperor Aurangzeb wished.

The Mughal chief, lulled by his own victory, was biding his time. When Firangji Narsala returned and met Shivaji, he apprised him of his interactions with Shaista Khan and of Khan's objective of capturing Shivaji.

Shivaji laughed, 'Firangji, let us show Shaista Khan that he should never mess with a mountain rat.'

It was while Shaista Khan was planning his next move that Shivaji pulled the rug right from under his feet. Shivaji, the Maratha warrior, hit out at Shaista Khan in such a smooth, spectacular and masterful manner that the Mughals forever labelled him as the 'Devil Incarnate'. With his inimitable courage, Shivaji sneaked into Shaista Khan's bedchambers in his harem (living quarters for women) and breached the circle of his bodyguards to attack and wound him.

It so happened that after his return from the military campaign, Shaista Khan had settled in Shivaji's old residence. This was not a grand palatial mansion but a simple yet strong and safe structure. There was a lot of room in the house as well as on the grounds for men, horses and other animals. Shaista Khan's men, his wives and slaves had all moved in with him into the house. The estate grounds housed his staff and stables. Further around the estate, his extensive army had put up their tents and started living. So, in a sense, Shaista Khan was living in Poona within a safely constructed circle comprising thousands of his guards and troops.

It was when Shivaji heard of Shaista Khan relaxing into a routine that he planned his next attack. He picked out a thousand of his bravest soldiers and left for the Mughal encampment. Other associates followed for support. This big army settled in villages all around the borders of Poona. Shivaji, with some three-hundred of his men, dressed in the Bijapuri army get-up and entered the enemy camp. They claimed to be sent as additional soldiers for Khan's army. Having being shown to their living quarters in the camp, Shivaji and his men settled down inconspicuously. It was the month of Ramadan and Shivaji knew that the army would break their fasts at sunset; have a lively feast and retire early. At midnight, when the attendants and guards had quietened, Shivaji and his men sneaked out and approached the palace.

Leadership Lesson #21

Never underestimate your enemy, no matter how small.

Shivaji had grown up in that very mansion. He knew each and every corner of the house. He knew exactly where Shaista Khan would be. Shivaji's team quickly sneaked through the kitchen quarters towards a secret pathway that led straight into the innermost master bedroom of the house.

Shivaji rushed through and entered the harem. He was followed by his three-hundred men at a quick pace. Shivaji headed straight to the enclosure that housed Shaista Khan's bed. The Mughal chief had already woken up to the shrieks of his wives and the scuffling around him. Just as he scrambled to get up and run, he saw Shivaji standing over him. Shivaji took a quick swipe at him with his sword and injured Shaista Khan on the waist. As Shaista Khan toppled over in pain, Shivaji took another swipe that lopped off three of his fingers. Then he quickly turned around and fought his way out of the chaos of Shaista Khan's bedchambers. On the way out, he killed Shaista Khan's son who was rushing in to protect his father.

By the time Mughal security personnel realised that the mansion had been infiltrated, Shivaji and his men were already on their way out. Along the way, the Marathas ransacked whatever they could see. Some of Shaista Khan's men were so shocked that they even tried to escape by jumping off balconies.

Legend says Goddess Tulja Bhavani gifted Shivaji the famous Bhavani sword. But that is a myth. The Portuguese gifted Shivaji Maharaj his ornate straight-bladed light sword, locally called 'firangi', because it was made by foreigners. The Chhatrapati added a special gem-studded hilt to it.

Among those who stayed back, some had to deal with their chief's injuries and make arrangements for transferring him to a safe place while the others ended up searching high and low for enemy forces rather than return the attack on them.

This *ganimikawa* (guerilla attack) was a success. The Marathas lost very few soldiers while the Mughals lost hundreds of men and Shaista Khan's son. Besides this, there was the matter of utter shame and ignominy because their chief had been personally attacked by Shivaji himself.

Shivaji had shown Emperor Aurangzeb the terror a 'mountain rat' could unleash. After Afzal Khan's killing, the attack on Shaista Khan made Shivaji a legend— a man of utmost courage, cunning and supernatural bravery. The story travelled far and wide, from the courts of Rajputs to the Nizams; from Golconda and Bijapur to the offices of the British, the Dutch and the Portuguese. The Maratha warrior's name started to be taken in fear and awe. The Mughal emperor was so miffed to hear about this humiliating attack that he instantly ordered for Shaista Khan to be demoted to Bengal forever.

Chapter 9

House Arrest in Agra

Just as the Mughals were recovering from the sneak attack on Shaista Khan, Shivba went on a rampage to loot the wealthy city of Surat in Gujarat. For five days, Shivba's men ransacked every business and factory in the city and held it to ransom.

Surat was a port city and a gateway to the Middle East, where lot of goods and money changed hands. It was full of businessmen and merchants. Because people were too busy conducting trade and transactions, the city also had very few secure areas. It had no walls or boundaries and unlimited money. The gates outside the homes of the rich were wholly useless. Even the rich and wealthy had no security guards protecting their wealth.

One morning, in 1664, the citizens of Surat received news that Shivaji was arriving to loot the town of its riches. Such was

Shivaji's legend at the time that people started running helter –skelter and found refuge wherever possible, leaving all their wealth ripe for picking. The Governor of Surat had no troops to defend his city and sent a messenger asking about the ransom.

Instead of discussing the ransom, Shivba detained the messenger and advanced upon the city. For five days, Shivba's men plundered Surat and stripped it of all the riches that they could lay their hands on. The rest of the city was burnt. Apart from the British and the Dutch, no one even stood up to the Marathas. It is said that Shivaji made away with riches worth almost a crore of rupees.

This action of Shivba was a direct affront to Emperor Aurangzeb. He immediately deputed Rajput Raja Jai Singh to corner Shivaji and teach him a lesson. Jai Singh arrived in Maharashtra with co-commander Diler Khan and around 50,000 troops to capture Poona and its nearby districts and forts. Jai Singh and Diler Khan pulled out all stops to defeat Shivaji and his people. The Mughal forces struck such terror in Maharashtra that for the sake of his people and peace and stability in his kingdom, Shivba had to finally write to the Mughal emperor and appeal to him for peace.

Intent on teaching Shivba a lesson, Jai Singh and Aurangzeb took months to agree to the terms and eventually took twenty-three forts from Shivaji, including Torna and Purandar. Emperor Aurangzeb also insisted that Shivaji agree to serve the Mughal regime in return for the protection of his people from further attacks by the Mughals. Shivba agree,d but under the condition that he be excused from having to present himself at

Emperor Aurangzeb's *darbar* like other Maratha and Deccan nobles. Even as a grown-up, Shivba didn't approve of bowing in front of anyone.

With this understanding, Shivba accompanied Diler Khan and Jai Singh on many battles against Bijapur. But even with those combined forces, the Mughal troops could not overturn the enemy in the Deccan. During these battles alongside the Mughals, Shivba became privy to several military insights. The first thing he realised was that the Mughal army was extremely disciplined and regimented. Everyone strictly followed instructions and they were heavily penalised if they did not. Shivba's second realisation was that even with all their army men and artillery, the Mughals were only competent in battle confrontations on a flat terrain. They were not at all adept on a hilly terrain and tended to get flustered very easily. That is why the Mughals experienced several failures in their battles in the south of India. Similarly, Shivba's army was not so confident on a flat terrain.

He therefore decided that it would be more strategic to focus on his expansion in the south where he had a distinct advantage over the strongest of his enemies, the Mughals. With this in mind, Shivba recommended to Emperor Aurangzeb

Leadership Lesson #22

Do not enter the enemy's lair without proper due diligence.

that he be appointed governor for the south on behalf of the Mughal empire.

Aurangzeb, fully aware of Shivba's ambitions, did not take the request too seriously. He was afraid that Shivba would eventually combine forces with Ahmednagar and Bijapur and strike out on his own.

But Jai Singh was wiser and better updated as to the goings-on in Deccan. Just then, as Shivba partnered with the Mughals against the Bijapuri forces, Shivba's military chief and oldest soldier, Netaji Palkar, had been lured away by higher pay and position. He had joined forces with Adil Shah. Therefore, Jai Singh was doubly aware of the crucial role Shivaji would play in retaining a Mughal stronghold in the south. If Shivaji also decided to join forces with Bijapur, all would be lost. He tried to convince the Maratha warrior to a diplomatic visit to Agra.

On the other hand, Shivba tried to persuade Raja Jai Singh about the idea of Hindavi Swarajya.

'*Raje*, do you know how the Mughals have been able to rule us for all these years? By dividing us and distracting us from our goals. These outsiders have just come and annexed our lands and are now employing us to fight with each other on their behalf. The Mughal emperor's army is, in fact, mostly a Rajput army. There are more powerful enemies like the Dutch, the Portuguese and the British waiting in the wings, once Mughal resources are spent. The common cause of Hindavi Swarajya, the uniting of all the people of Hindustan to be self-ruled is the need of the hour,' suggested Shivba.

'Shivaji *Raje*, I understand your point of view. But I am a Rajput and have given my word to the emperor. I am allied with the Mughals for many strategic motives. I am unable to break this alliance. Your position, in the south of the subcontinent, is very important. The emperor has to understand that he cannot be successful in his plans unless he has you to control the other kingdoms. An alliance with the Mughals will come with several benefits to you and your people. I will myself put in a word on your behalf to Emperor Aurangzeb but I recommend that you come to our capital in Agra and formally approach him with this request,' Jai Singh, who had come to admire Shivba after they had fought together against Bijapur, said.

Shivba replied, 'Going to Agra is extremely risky for me. I do not trust the Mughals on their own homeland.'

Jai reassured him. 'Do not worry, *Raje*. I will personally ensure your safety in Agra. It is a Rajput who is giving his word to you,' he said.

Shivba agreed and set out for Agra along with his young son Sambhaji; a small group of his men and a hundred or so soldiers, as required for a formal visit. Jijabai added a warning to her blessings as Shivba touched her feet before his departure.

'Shivba, be careful of the Mughals. Do not trust anyone. Do not eat anything without testing it. You are meeting an emperor who killed his own brothers in his quest for power. In times of trouble, keep your faith in Goddess Tulja Bhavani,' she said.

Then she turned to bless Shivba's close companion and bodyguard, Hiroji Farzand. 'Do not leave my son's side. Be with him like a shadow,' she said.

'Do not worry, *Aaisaheb*. I will be careful and prepared. Hiroji will always keep me company,' Shivba reassured his mother with a smile before he finally took off.

He was hoping that the visit would enable him to gather some invaluable information about the Mughal empire—how the emperor managed governance matters of such a large, spread-out kingdom; how he kept his men in line, how he decided on policy matters, etc. Shivba wanted to see how all this could be applied to his model and vision of Hindavi Swarajya.

He and his group of bodyguards reached Agra around the same time that Aurangzeb was celebrating his newly-anointed kingship. Artists and musicians had arrived from all over the empire. The palace was in the throes of preparation to receive the emperor in his *darbar*. Although Jai Singh was not personally present, his son Ram Singh had been sent to welcome Shivba to the royal palace.

Shivba and his son Sambhaji were received by the Mughal prime minister and led to the *Diwan-e-Khaas* (the VIP *darbar*) to meet Emperor Aurangzeb. Shivba greeted and presented his gifts to Aurangzeb. The emperor received the gifts but flicked his fingers indicating to his men that the Maratha warrior be

Leadership Lesson #23

Do not take an insult lying down. Dignity and pride are everything to a human being.

led away. Shivba was surprised at being taken to the place where nobles in the *darbar* stood. It was not where important people were placed. He was taken way behind where nobles of a much lower rank stood and where the emperor could not even see him in court.

Shivba was stung. He realised that being moved like that was meant to be an insult. Offended, he raised his voice and complained about the treatment meted out to a king like him.

Aurangzeb, satisfied at having offended Shivba, immediately motioned for Jai Singh's son Ram Singh to pacify him. But on seeing Shivba refusing to be mollified, the emperor ordered for Shivba and Sambhaji to be taken away and placed under house arrest at Ram Singh's residence.

Jai Singh rushed to Agra to mediate on the matter.

'*Badshah*, Shivaji *Raje* is in Agra to meet you at my insistence and assurance. We cannot place him under house arrest like this,' he urged the emperor.

'Jai Singh, he is the one who took offence at a simple court matter. Besides, Shivaji arriving here at this point of time is a political opportunity we simply must take advantage of ... if you know what I mean,' Aurangzeb insinuated slyly.

Jai Singh knew what he meant. The emperor wanted to take the opportunity to kill Shivaji while he was on their territory.

Shivaji Maharaj was around 5 feet 6 inches tall and moderately built compared to his Deccan and Mughal enemies, who were much taller and heftier.

'As a Rajput, I have given Shivaji my word that he will be taken care of. I will never allow that to happen,' Jai Singh promised and left. He knew that the emperor wasn't loyal to anyone. But he also knew that he wouldn't try and attack a king like Shivaji and offend the Rajputs without adequate justification, immediately after his own coronation as *Badshah*.

Yet, Aurangzeb was not a man to be trusted. Jai Singh sent a message to Shivba's men through their spies.

Read on to find out how Shivba managed to escape the clutches of the Mughal emperor.

Chapter 10

Escape from Agra

Jai Singh sent a message to Shivba's men through their spies. He apprised Shivba of the danger he was in and asked him to lay low till they found some way out of this situation. Shivba decided to follow the Rajput leader's advice till he could devise a way to escape house arrest. Right after, Shivba and Sambhaji were shifted sneakily to a house at an unknown location. At the time, Aurangzeb had posted twenty guards outside the main door of this large house, ten guards on the floor which Shivba and Sambhaji occupied and four right outside their bedchambers. Although Shivba and Sambhaji were not cuffed, neither were they allowed to step outside nor could they have any visitors without prior permission. They were under arrest in Agra for two to three months before Shivba found a creative way to escape.

A couple of weeks after his house arrest began, Shivba pretended to be violently ill. Prevaricating that his illness was contagious, Shivba asked all his followers to be sent away. In reality, they were sent away to prepare for the eventual escape. He then requested the royal police to permit him to send out sweets and fruits blessed by his hands to the poor and underprivileged. He was supposedly seeking their goodwill for a quick recovery. The police, knowing this to be a routine practice by noblemen, took this request to the emperor. Aurangzeb allowed it under the condition that every trunk or container be inspected carefully before it was allowed to be blessed and taken away.

'Make sure that every container is checked thoroughly. Shivaji is a wily warrior. He could smuggle in weapons through those containers and spring a sudden attack in the middle of the night. Do not take this lightly,' warned Aurangzeb.

And so, it started. Every noon, two containers of fruits and sweets would arrive in the corridor outside Shivba's bedchambers. Hiroji would bring out a frail-looking Shivba to touch and bless the two containers and do a small *pooja* with some *diyas* (lights), *dhoop* and *agarbattis* (incense sticks). The containers would then be sent off with the men to *dargahs* and temples in Agra. The checking would be strict.

Leadership Lesson #24

If an opponent is disciplined, wear him down with time.

Every evening, a guard would come inside Shivba's bedchamber and check on the king lying in bed, coughing, and leave. Because of Shaista Khan, everyone had heard about Shivaji and his guerilla warfare techniques. Every day, the soldiers would comb through the containers to check if there were any weapons or unwanted objects in them. There would, of course, be nothing. Week in, week out, the same thing would happen.

Everyday the guards would look at the containers thoroughly and then witness Shivba's stooped form hobbling to touch them, perfoming *pooja* and sending them away. The guard in the afternoon would even smile and wonder at the emperor's paranoia—how could this small, frail man lying in bed and coughing so hoarsely attack them and escape from here? It was impossible. Soon, absolutely reassured that Shivba's health was deteriorating daily, the guards relaxed a bit.

Within just a couple of weeks, the checking of the containers became cursory, a mere formality. The emperor also didn't bother much knowing that Shivba's health was worsening. The afternoon guard would also not probe too much if he found Shivba sleeping, covered in his blankets and breathing or coughing heavily.

Leadership Lesson #25

Groom yourself to be totally unpredictable. Do the opposite of what the opponent expects.

One day, as intended, Shivba and Sambhaji took the opportunity to hide inside the containers and be taken away outside the palace, courtesy the lax checks. The house guards were unaware of this escape because of the periodic coughing sounds emanating from the bedchambers. The afternoon guard saw Hiroji Farzand huddled in a blanket, breathing heavily. Shivba's royal bracelet shone on his hand outside the covers, assuring the guard that his captive was very much where he was supposed to be.

A couple of hours later, Hiroji and his assistant told the guards that they had to urgently get some medicines for their chief. They asked them not to disturb him in his sleep and left to never return. Suspicious at the complete silence in the bedroom after several hours, the guards entered the room to investigate. They found two bolsters covered with a blanket instead of Shivaji! Neither the son nor the other bodyguards were anywhere to be seen.

The guards went in search of the containers to the *dargahs* and temples where they had been donated. The containers had reached but the men were nowhere to be seen. Emperor Aurangzeb was angry at this deception and sent out his men in search the very next morning. Knowing that Shivaji and Sambhaji were on foot, his men caught hold of every man and child travelling to Maharashtra.

However, by then, Shivba and his son had taken on the guise of a travelling *sadhu* and his disciple. They dressed in saffron and covered their faces with ash as was the norm for holy men at the time. The duo had set out in the the opposite direction and were headed towards Allahabad instead of Maharashtra. After a certain point, the duo split up. Shivba's spies spread the rumour of his passing. Sambhaji was sent home with some trusted bodyguards while Shivba travelled alone for a month before arriving back in Maharashtra.

It is said that Jijabai was consulting with a few ministers on some official matter when a *sadhu* entered her chambers chanting '*Alak Niranjan*' and '*Om Shanti Om*'. She was alarmed to see a stranger in her private rooms before she took a closer look. She realised that it was none other than her Shivba who had pulled himself out of the clutches of the emperor and returned home safely. It is said that all of Maharashtra rejoiced at this homecoming and celebrated for weeks.

Aurangzeb was terribly furious and disappointed at Shivaji's escape from his captivity. He believed in keeping a tight check over his people and his administration. Shivaji's escape from Agra, right from under his nose, reflected negligence and carelessness in the Mughal administration. Emperor Aurangzeb was ashamed of it and took this regret to his grave.

Chapter 11

Battle of Sinhagadh

Shivaji's escape from Agra had caused a lot of embarrassment for Raja Jai Singh in Aurangzeb's court. His former support and backing for Shivaji now seemed like collusion to the emperor. His subsequent defeat in battles with Bijapur made him persona non grata in Agra. In the very next few months, he was replaced by Aurangzeb's son, Prince Muazzam, as the Governor of Aurangabad.

The prince, famous for his love for hunting and animal fights, was not known for his military acumen. His appointment brought some relief to Shivaji. Besides this, the Mughal military had to concentrate their energies to fend off an attack from Persian enemies. Aurangzeb also had to undertake some drastic cost-cutting measures in the aftermath of heavy losses from continuous battles.

Shivaji took this reprieve to organise his own administration. He used this period of peace to organise his power on the western coast against Bijapur and the Siddis of Janjira. After Raja Jai Singh passed away, Shivaji also sent emissaries to the Mughal empire to show his peaceful intentions. He also offered to send his son Sambhaji to serve under the emperor. But his moves were not acknowledged. Although the emperor recognised the Maratha and his power, none of the twenty-three forts he had surrendered as part of the Treaty of Purandar were restored to him.

Shivba, therefore, focussed on minding his own business and refrained from resuming hostilities with either Bijapur or Delhi for the time being. Instead, he went about setting laws and regulations for his kingdom that have created benchmarks for policymaking in India.

The Marathas, the people of Shivaji, who had lost lives, limbs and property in all the upheaval and chaos from wars with the Mughals, thrived and prospered during this respite. With the knowledge that Mughal soldiers came with a different sort of discipline, conditioning and inherent skills, Shivba also hired many of the soldiers that Aurangzeb made redundant with his cost-cutting measures. Shivba waited and watched Muazzam. Knowing that the emperor was too busy and broke to react quickly, Shivba set about planning to correct a few wrongs. Biding his time, he made a few quick attempts to grab some of the forts that were taken from him.

The most daring among them was the overnight conquest of Kondana. It so happened that Jijabai and Shivba were living at Rajgarh then. The Treaty of Purandar, although a need of the time, weighed heavily on Jijabai's heart. The surrender of their forts to the Mughals did not sit right with her. Every evening, during her prayers at sunset atop Rajgarh fort, she would eye Kondana wistfully in the far distance. On one such evening, Shivaji's top lieutenant and one of his closest friends—Tanaji Malusare—had visited Jijabai to invite her to his son's wedding. He had joined Jijabai in her evening prayers and saw her looking at Kondana with moist eyes.

'*Aaisaheb*, do I see tears in your eyes? What is it that is making you so sad? What can I do to allay this sadness,' asked Tanaji with concern.

'On a clear day such as this, one can see Kondana fort in all its glory. But to me, it is a picture of what we Marathas lost to those Mughals. Of all the forts we had to surrender, that is the one that causes me the most despair. If there is one thing you can do as a son, it is this—you must restore Kondana back to me,' said Jijabai wiping her tears.

'*Aaisaheb*, *Raje* is biding his time for his next battles. We cannot be impulsive,' urged Tanaji.

'Tanaji, if you must be patient, so be it. However, remember the weight and misery borne by your mother's heart each day Kondana remains in Mughal control,' said Jijabai and left the prayer room.

Leadership Lesson #26

Listen to your inner voice. Your instincts can sometimes be your best guide.

Tanaji felt miserable with this curt dismissal. He met with Shivaji and apprised him of Jijabai's wishes. Shivaji assured him that maintaining peace was the right approach and sent him off to plan his son's upcoming nuptials.

However, the matter weighed on both their minds. Jijabai's wish was an order and neither of them could just dismiss it. Just a few days later, despite his inner voice balking at the risk of it, Shivaji started planning on how to capture Kondana in the best manner possible. He brought out his best team to figure out a plan of action. They tried to compute if they could pull off a surprise attack in the middle of the night and wrest control of the fort from their sleep-addled enemies. However, Kondana is almost 4,300 feet in height and an extremely steep fort to climb. Besides, it was managed by the very brave and strong Rajput leader, Udaybhan Singh.

Somehow, Tanaji came to know of Shivba's idea to recapture Kondana and left his son's wedding to rush back to Rajgarh and join the team.

'*Raje*, why did you leave me out of planning such an important battle? Do you not consider me deserving of this challenge?' asked an offended Tanaji.

'Of course not, you misunderstand me, Tanaji. I already have a lot of misgivings about this venture. I merely thought you were needed more at your son's wedding,' explained Shivaji.

> Although he founded his Swarajya in 1646, he crowned himself king only in 1674 at forty-four. He died merely six years later.

'*Aadhi lagna Kondaanyaache!* (I will plan Kondana's wedding first!). Let's do this tomorrow itself; it is predicted to be a dark night,' declared the brave Tanaji and left to plan his battle strategy.

He rounded up some local guides who knew the hill like the back of their hand and around 300 men. He also brought his pet monitor lizard, Yashwanti, for the campaign. Monitor lizards were domesticated very frequently then. Their sharp and sticky paws help them to cling to mountain sides and scale up quickly. Mavlas often hung a thick rope tied around these creatures and used them to get a hold and anchor themselves better on a rope ladder when climbing steep mountains. The lizards would quickly cling to the wall of the mountains and provide a way up for the soldiers.

Yashwanti was sent up to anchor herself on the cliff for climbing support. It is said that when she couldn't anchor herself correctly even after a couple of tries, Tanaji beseeched her with these words.

'Yashwanti, take me up these fort walls and help me win back Kondana for our Jijamata. I cannot bear to see tears in her eyes,' he urged her quietly.

Eventually, all the soldiers nimbly climbed the hill and advanced into the gates. With a shrill cry of 'Har Har

Leadership Lesson #27

What you gain is not important if it means the loss of a loved one.

Mahadev', Tanaji's men surprise attacked the sleep- and opium-addled Mughal soldiers. Udaybhan's men gave a tough yet desperate fight to defend the fort. Udaybhan himself fought and lost his life but not before he had slain the brave Tanaji. The Maratha men were momentarily disheartened at seeing their leader fallen. But soon, Tanaji's brother Suryaji took the lead and secured the fort. Around a thousand Rajput soldiers were killed either in battle or while trying to climb down the fort walls. The Marathas rushed to set fire to enemy tents to send a signal to Shivaji at Rajgarh about the recapture of the fort.

Shivba and Jijabai rejoiced at Rajgarh till news of Tanaji's sacrifice reached them. 'I should never have gone ahead with this risky campaign. *Gadh aala pan sinha gela* (We have won the fort but lost the lion). Let Kondana be heretofore called Sinhagadh in memory of the man who fought like a lion and sacrificed his life for it,' declared Shivaji.

Chapter 12

Shivaji Gets Crowned King

Shivaji's return from the clutches of the Mughal regime gave him a sort of cult hero status. *Powadas* and folk songs were composed about Shivba as a hero who fought the Mughals; about Shivba's courage and audacity in battle and the cunning stratagem he employed while escaping from Agra. The imaginations of the Maratha people had been captured by the spirit of Swarajya by then. They were hopeful that Shivaji would be the hero who would deliver the promised Hindavi Swarajya.

On a more pragmatic front, Shivaji's territory had expanded; he had groomed and developed a strong army and navy. Although he was a king in public perception and imagination; his royalty would not be acknowledged by the Mughals, the Bijapuris and the Nizam Shahi till he was crowned the king of Maharashtra. The experience at the Mughal court, where Shivba had to stand among other noblemen far below his stature, was a case in point. He needed a formal coronation so as to be perceived as a *Raja* who enjoyed equal political stature as other royalty.

Besides, on a local administrative level, his promises to his subjects—treaties or understanding; conference of land or titles and legal ownership of the territories he acquired—could not have sanctity without the seal of royalty. Jijabai and Shivba's council of ministers felt that Swarajya needed to be established and his kingship had to be validated publicly so that the intellectuals in society confirmed Shivba's rise as the only hero of Hindavi Swarajya and his title as the only Chhatrapati (emperor).

However, it was not that easy a task. Casteism was much more rampant in Indian society then than it is in modern times. According to caste strictures, only a pure Kshatriya could be crowned king and demand the loyalty of his subjects. Traditionally, the Bhonsles had humble origins—they were tillers of the soil who went on to become *sardars* and *zamindars* after being rewarded for their bravery in battle by various kings. The conservative and short-sighted Brahmins of the time did not acknowledge Shivaji's claim to royalty and therefore refused to participate and validate his coronation.

Leadership Lesson #28

A leader has to think beyond himself. He has to think of his team and his goal.

Shivaji himself was a progressive leader. Jijabai was tremendously secular in her religious and social beliefs, patronising several Hindu, Sikh as well as Muslim saints. Her son shared all those beliefs. His army and council of ministers was inclusive with members of many castes, communities and religions. Shivaji was also an extremely pragmatic and goal-oriented leader. This meant that performance towards a goal was the only quality he admired and rewarded in his team.

Instead of feeling offended, he took the refusal of the Brahmins to acknowledge his coronation as a minor hindrance. In his wisdom, he understood fully that religion and ritualism were more than just dogma. They had to be interpreted in the right context for the welfare of many. He had no doubt that he deserved to be king. If the local Brahmins did not deem him to fit to be king over some technicality, he would find someone with the best credentials who did.

He sent out his men to Benares, the hotbed of the Hindu spiritual world to look for a priest who would agree to preside over and officiate his coronation. This wise priest was Shri Gaga Bhatta, a learned man who was an expert in the four Vedas and Hindu spiritual texts. He agreed to come to Maharashtra and officiate the proceedings in a manner suitable for a Kshatriya prince.

Gaga Bhatta announced a *muhurat* (auspicious time). Other lavish arrangements were then planned. By nature, unlike royalty in those days, Shivba was not at all a self-indulgent, pleasure-seeking king. In fact, he lived an austere and disciplined life with a distaste for over-indulgence.

He had several discussions with his ministers on the matter.

'It is a mere formality. The money spent on it would be better used for the welfare of the poor and needy in our kingdom,' said Shivaji.

'*Raje*, we do agree. You know we will not disobey you. However, a coronation and subsequent celebrations are also expected by the people. It will be a matter of pride for the people to see you crowned as Chhatrapati. It will be as good as a festival for the public. Do they not have a right to celebrate the Swarajya they so wished for?' countered one of his ministers.

When Shivaji still did not agree, Jijabai stepped in.

'Shivba, the wishes of our people are what have given you the power to set up Swarajya for the land of Marathas. Should we not celebrate that? Besides, these celebrations are not only for ourselves. Think of all the alms-giving, the charity, the feasts for the poor and needy that will be part of the revelry. Think of your poor, frail old mother who has lived a long life of eighty years only so she could see this day,' Jijabai teased him with a smile.

Shivaji could brook no further argument. Jijabai's health was indeed frail and her wishes could not be ignored. He went with his officers to welcome Gaga Bhatta to Maharashtra and participated in all the preparations. Not being of a royal family himself, Shivba was keen to understand the intricacies of regal practices and etiquette of kings and courts across the country. He had always been impressed with the Vijaynagar empire in the south, the Rajputs in Rajasthan and King Kantirava Narasa Raja from Mysore. He asked for a lot of research to be done on their royal courtly practices which he would emulate in his own kingdom. Shivaji also followed Narasa Raja's example and launched a coin in his own name—Shivrai—after his own coronation. Invitations started being prepared.

Thousands of people—nobles, tradespeople, sardars, zamindars, soldiers and chieftains—were invited months in advance. Daily feasts were organised for lakhs of people in honour of the Chhatrapati. Shivaji began the coronation rituals by first visiting the Parshuram temple in Chiplun and then his family deity Bhavani Devi at Pratapgarh, to seek her blessings.

He then atoned for the sins he had and would commit in his lifetime by weighing himself on a balance and giving away an equivalent weight of clothing, grains, fruits, copper, silver and gold to the poor and needy in the kingdom.

The day of the coronation dawned bright and early. Shivba began his day by bowing to his spiritual guru, Shri Ramdas Swami and his mother, and began the proceedings. For Jijabai, it was the happiest day of her life when all her dreams of Swarajya for her dear Shivba had been realised.

Shivba then touched the feet of Gaga Bhatta and the other Brahmins who were to officiate the coronation and gifted them their alms. He was then, like all kings, offered an *abhishek* (water, flowers and milk are poured on the head) and then taken for a bath in holy water. Shivaji then dressed in a rich red-and-gold coloured robe; put on golden ornaments; donned a royal turban and wore his royal sword. After that, he was led to his grand throne with great fanfare amid a lot of holy chanting and lights. His wife, Soyrabai, sat next to him while his heir Sambhaji sat behind with Shivaji's *ashta pradhan mandal* (council of eight mnisters). He was surrounded in all directions by people holding diyas to ward off evil. Gaga Bhatta approached Shivaji and held the royal golden parasol over his head and proclaimed him—Chhatrapati Shivaji Maharaj.

It is reported that every cannon in every fort in the kingdom was fired at the same time to announce to the world that Shivaji had been anointed Chhatrapati.

After he had been blessed by all the wise and learned men in his court, on Jijabai's instructions, Shivba sat on an elephant and proceeded to meet the people of his land. The royal procession, with its saffron flag aloft, traversed the gaily-painted streets to meet subjects who were rejoicing outside their freshly-decorated houses. He was showered with flowers, rice grains and scented water. Women and children on the streets were all given some gift or another.

'*Aaisaheb* would have been proud to see all the love showered on me in this procession. She has always dreamed of a Swarajya where the people are as happy as this. I will

Leadership Lesson #29

Don't get stuck with dogma. Where there is a will, there is always a way out.

do everything in my power to maintain this prosperity in my Swarajya. If her health was better, she could have seen all this herself,' Shivaji rued.

It is said that Shivaji's throne was studded with gold and gems and would cost almost Rs 14,00,000 in today's age. The Chhatrapati also gave away vast sums of money and gifts of every kind to the general public. Shivba's first act as king was to abolish the Persian titles of the officers and soldiers in his court and re-honour them with Sanskrit titles. It is said that the coronation cost more than a crore of rupees with more than half of it being given away to the needy. It almost emptied the treasury, it is said. But Shivba was happy and satisfied to have celebrated his coronation in the exact manner expected by Jijabai. The matriarch was eighty when she died unexpectedly, just a few weeks after the coronation. She witnessed her dream—of seeing Shivaji become king and establish Hindavi Swarajya for his people—come true.

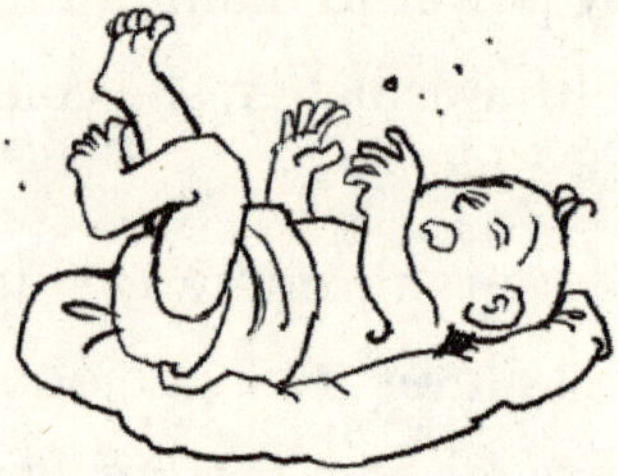

Chapter 13

The Legend of Hirkani

And that was how Jijabai's young Shivba became Maharashtra's pride, Chhatrapati Shivaji Maharaj. Through the land, people rejoiced and told stories about their favourite hero and how he fought his enemies to win Swarajya for his people. Chhatrapati Shivaji brought about an assimilation of the best practices of kingdoms around the subcontinent and adopted new practices and policies that not only set an example for the royalty in those days but also laid the foundation for the republic that India modelled itself around. There were quite a few legends that people built around Shivaji Maharaj, the iconic brave Maratha warrior, from the time of his reign. One of those legends was that of Hirkani, the milkmaid.

Due to Jijabai's rather impressive upbringing, Shivaji Maharaj always respected women. Unlike other kings and nawabs of the day, Shivaji's men never killed or disrespected women and children after a battle. Innocent civilians surviving a battle were always allowed to leave. In fact, Shivaji harshly penalised many of his soldiers for breaking this law.

'Shivba, any country or society prospers only when the women of that country or society are safe and secure. It is the women who take care of and feed the families that give us our soldiers, our teachers, our officers and so on. A king's main duty is to run his country in such a way that the women in his kingdom live with safety and dignity,' she often used to say.

The story of Hirkani is not just a simple folktale. It is an ode to the bravery and love of a mother for her baby that forced a strict but compassionate king to reconsider his own rules for the welfare of his people. It is the story of a poor milkmaid who lived during the reign of Chhatrapati Shivaji Maharaj.

Since 1674 when Shivaji *Raje* first seized it, the Raigad fort has had a special place in Maratha history. It was surrounded by a thick jungle at the very top of a peak in the Western Ghats in Maharashtra. This fort also has massive, thick walls to protect it from enemies and stormy weather on three sides and a steep, sheer cliff drop into the ghats on the fourth side. Who would be crazy enough to try and climb up or down this steep drop?

Leadership Lesson #30

Rules are meant to protect people and facilitate functioning. If a rule doesn't benefit either, the rule should be modified.

Hirkani was a poor milkmaid who lived at the foothills of the famous fort. Her husband was a soldier, often at war in some camp out of town. She lived in the village at the base of this large fort and supplemented the family income by selling milk and milk products. The village was the main source of supplies for the daily needs of noblemen and guards living in the fort above. The villagers had to climb up the road to the fort's gates with their goods and sell them door to door.

However, the large, heavy gates of Raigad opened only at dawn and shut at dusk every day. Since it was considered risky to be out and about in the night in the jungle around the fort, the guards were forbidden from opening the gates for anyone after sunset till the next morning.

Like many of her village neighbours, Hirkani would also stand in line at the main gates with her milk containers every morning, waiting to enter and sell the milk to the residents of the fort. The work suited her. She had a toddler who she left in the care of her old mother-in-law. She would leave early in the morning, while her baby was still asleep, to reach the top of the fort and deliver her milk orders. She would then have a quiet lunch of *jhunka bhakar* with her friends from the village under the shade of a tree; run some errands for her customers at the fort that made her some more money and then rush home late in the afternoon, just in time to play with her baby and cook dinner.

One day though, Hirkani's day didn't proceed as per plan. Before leaving for work in the morning, Hirkani's baby was cranky, as babies often are when they are teething, and refused to let her go to work. She somehow reassured her baby that she would return soon and left for work. She had a hundred things to do that day.

Somehow, Hirkani managed to reach the fort but she was late and took longer to get into the fort. She rushed to finish her work for the day but kept getting delayed at every turn. Soon, she realised she was going to be very late in reaching home. But she still had to rush to the medicine man in the fort to get some medicine for her baby's teething pains. She knew her baby would sleep peacefully with the herbal medicine. When she reached there, she found that there was a queue at the pharmacy too. Unfortunately, by the time she had bought the teething medicine, she heard the big iron gates of the Raigad fort clanging shut.

She had to get home!

Hirkani's baby was home and she was stuck on the fort! She rushed to the gates and pleaded with the Mavla (soldier) at the security gate to open it and let her pass. But the security guard was loyal to his king and refused to break the rules for anyone.

When the Mavla refused to listen to her pleas and relent, the thought of her baby experiencing teething pains and sorely missing her began plaguing Hirkani. Suddenly, she decided to do something very drastic and risky.

As a child, Hirkani and her friends would walk through the jungle and climb parts of the hill up to a certain altitude when they played during the day while grazing their cows and sheep. She had won several bets with her friends running up and down the hill through the jungle.

Hirkani was slightly familiar with the terrain. She was also quick and agile on her feet. She decided she was not going to wait around for the gates to open at sunrise while her poor baby waited for her. She quietly sneaked around the gate and started climbing down the steep drop in the hillside down to her village.

It was dark and the drop was very dangerous. One wrong step and Hirkani would have fallen to her death. But she focussed on reaching home. As she climbed down, slid and tumbled through the shrubs and grass on that dangerous hillside, she had only one thought in her mind. 'My baby needs me. I need to get home safe for my baby.'

Her eventual descent to the bottom of the cliff left her severely scratched, wounded and hurt from multiple wounds. Her saree was all dusty and her limbs were shaking. But one smile from her baby and all her sorrows melted away.

She hugged her baby, applied the teething medicine and the duo went to sleep.

Like every day, the following day Hirkani woke up early and left for work. Her baby was sleeping soundly because of the medicine. However, the Mavla at the gates was shocked

Leadership Lesson #31

A leader has to be emphathetic and compassionate towards all his followers.

to see Hirkani back, gaining entry into the fort this time! He remembered her arguing with him the previous evening, wanting to leave the fort.

He took Hirkani to Chhatrapati's court. He passionately complained to the Maharaj about how Hirkani broke the fort's rules and escaped from the clifftop, demanding that she be punished severely. But, to the Mavla's surprise, instead of getting angry, the king only listened sympathetically. This was another instance of considering a crime in the right context for Shivba. The Chhatrapati examined Hirkani's multiple scratches and bruises and asked her about how she climbed down such a dangerous terrain.

Adventure and rappelling about in the hills was not new for Shivaji. He and his friends had done it a thousand times. But he also knew that they would not risk such an activity in the middle of the night.

'Only a mother would go to such great lengths to reach her baby. It is only maternal love that will force a woman to take such a terrible risk for the welfare of her child,' he thought worriedly.

He was full of admiration and appreciation of Hirkani's bravery and her dedication to her baby, but also felt concern. He praised her for her courage. But for the safety of others in his kingdom, in case they tried such suicidal adventures, Chhatrapati Shivaji first relaxed the rules of gate closure during emergency situations. He then ordered for a wall to be built at the site of the unprotected vertical drop and named it the Hirkani *Buruj*!

This *buruj* (monument) still exists near Raigad fort, and the story of Hirkani remains an inspiration for all mothers in India, who move mountains, or climb down them, for their children.

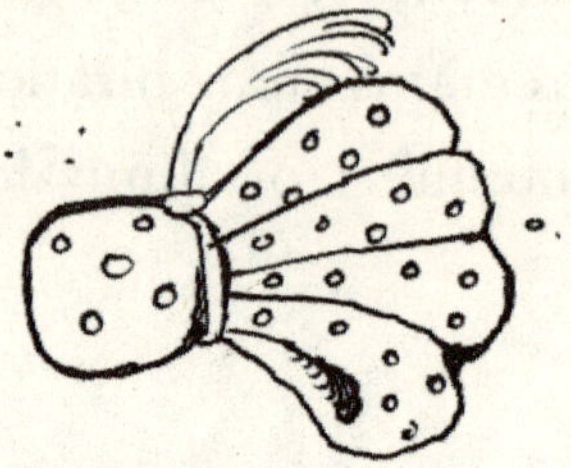

Chapter 14

Waghya's Loyalty

Another folk legend related to Chhatrapati Shivaji Maharaj and the Raigad fort that is often told and retold as a testament to loyalty is the story of Waghya. Although history books have no factual references to Waghya or his importance in Chhatrapati Shivaji Maharaj's life, it is an endearing story nonetheless.

This story is about King Shivaji and his faithful and most loyal friend, Waghya, his pet dog. Waghya was a mongrel, sable black in colour, and the Chhatrapati's constant companion at the Raigad fort.

No one really knows how the king came to adopt Waghya. Especially since Maharaj would often be away from home for long stretches of time on battle campaigns. But it is said that the Chhatrapati often stepped out incognito into his kingdom. He would go to the main bazaars or the public chowks in his kingdom, dressed in a dhoti and vest, disguised as a regular citizen. At such times, he would use a blanket so that it partially covered his face. He would do this to find out the ground reality in his kingdom. As a layman, the Chhatrapati would mingle with his people in public places to gauge what was really happening with his subjects. He would casually gather information on whether citizens faced any difficulties or challenges; whether prices of food were affordable; which officers from his administration were corrupt, and so on.

Once, when Chhatrapati Shivaji was coming home late through the wilderness from such an outing, he saw a huge, ferocious dog growling and bearing down on a small, black pup. It was late at night and the forest path was otherwise quiet. The puppy was scared and shaking but brave enough to stand his ground even as the large dog came charging upon him. The Chhatrapati found the pup's behaviour very intriguing. The pup refused to run away or break eye contact with the big dog even when his life was clearly in peril.

Shivaji Maharaj stopped and watched this tense standoff between the two creatures with amusement. Then, fearing that the larger dog would attack the small pup, Shivaji quickly threw the small stick in his hand at the big dog to scare him.

Leadership Lesson #32

Loyalty begets loyalty. Protectiveness begets protection.

As soon as the stick hit the big dog, he turned and growled fiercely at the king. But he took the hint and skulked away. The small pup was still on his guard though. He kept looking warily at the king.

The Chhatrapati resumed his walk towards his fort. But he heard a small rustling behind him. He ignored it. After a little while, he felt a small tug on the blanket he was carrying on his shoulder. He looked behind to see the black puppy following him.

He thought the pup would leave once he reached his palace. His guards would definitely not allow it in. But when Shivaji reached his private chambers, he realised that the puppy had slipped past all the security guards and continued to tail him.

Amused, he asked his personal guards to give the pup some food and take it away. However, when Shivaji woke up the next day, he was surprised to see the pup at the foot of his bed.

All through the day, the Chhatrapati tried shaking off the black pup but to no avail. Somehow, the puppy always found his way back to the king. Over the next few days, the king was surprised to see that the pup would follow him almost everywhere and stand guard. Soon, the king realised that it was not easy to intimidate the pup. He was impressed with the

Leadership Lesson #33

It is not size that makes a man brave and courageous. It is fearlessness and conviction.

courage with which the scrawny pup stood his ground fiercely instead of running away when in danger. Shivaji liked this quality in people. Soon the pup became the cause of much amusement among the Maharaj's entourage and foot soldiers. No matter how much they tried to send him off, the puppy refused to budge.

One fine day, amused at his growling on being scared by the palace guards, the Chhatrapati declared, 'It is not size but fearlessness and conviction to stand his ground that makes a man brave. This pup is incredibly courageous and loyal. Although he is a small dog, he has the heart of a fearless tiger. We will call him Waghya from now on.'

Waghya became the Chhatrapati's constant companion. Over the next few months, the puppy grew into a fine, young dog with long, floppy ears and a black shiny coat. He would accompany the king to his *taalim* (fitness workouts), *darbar* (court), meals and meetings. He would sit outside the dining room when the king ate and ate his own food only after his master was done. He would lie at the foot of the king's bed all night, alert to the slightest movement outside the chambers. When the king had to go for a tour, Waghya would mope around the king's chambers and refuse to eat his meals till his master returned.

Perhaps it was gratitude for protecting him from a dangerous situation, but through all the ups and downs in the Chhatrapati's life, Waghya remained steadfastly by his side. In those days, when courtiers played politics to retain control in *darbar* as well as through the conflict for power brewing at the time between Shivaji Maharaj's son Sambhaji and his second wife Soyrabai, Maharaj found Waghya's affection and loyalty very endearing.

One day, Shivaji fell ill due to food poisoning. He was only fifty at the time but his health deteriorated quickly within just a week.

As the Chhatrapati lay sick during those last days, Waghya never left his side. He would prompt the helpers to come when the king needed changing or some water to drink. He would devotedly keep pacing around his bed, checking up on the king. When Chhatrapati breathed his last after almost a fortnight of sickness, Waghya sat quietly by his body till the final arrangements had been made.

Most of the palace guards and family knew that Waghya would take the king's death to heart. He had followed the king even on his final procession to the cremation ground. But none of them were prepared for Waghya's reaction when he saw his master on the funeral pyre. When Waghya saw the pyre on which his master's body lay being lit up, he leapt across and immolated himself.

Over the centuries, Waghya's devotion and loyalty to Chhatrapati Shivaji Maharaj has become a legend. A few decades ago, some locals built a statue at a site near the Raigad fort to commemorate Waghya's legend—an endearing story of friendship between a dog and Maharashtra's king of kings.

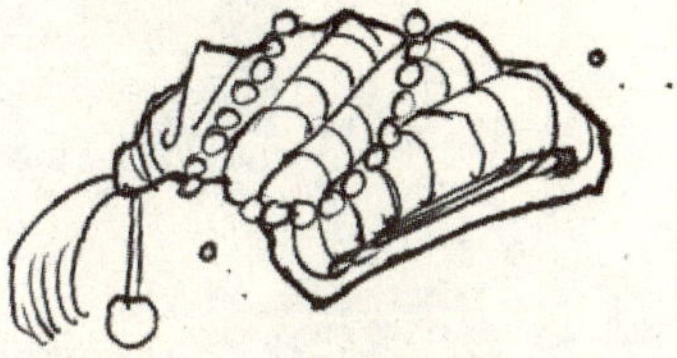

Chapter 15

The Legacy of Chhatrapati Shivaji Maharaj

Jijabai's words were to come true. Her son, Shivba, did make her immensely proud. He made Maharashtra proud.

Chhatrapati Shivaji Maharaj's death didn't dim his legacy. Instead, his vision of Swarajya fuelled the spark of independence and self-respect in the hearts of millions of Indians for centuries. It is true that many of India's freedom fighters and revolutionaries like Bhagat Singh were inspired by Shivaji's courage and vision. It is also said that Indian nationalist and freedom fighter Subhash Chandra Bose was inspired by the courageous stories of Shivaji's escape from Agra and used a similar tactic to escape house arrest by the British, under disguise.

There have been many kings in Indian history who have been as brave, dashing and courageous. Yet, their stories have

never inspired generations of countryfolk the same way that Shivaji Maharaj's have. Chhatrapati Shivaji Maharaj's true legend has more to do with his pragmatic, people-friendly policies than his courage and daring in the battlefield. Like a Sanskrit *subhashita* says, 'A good king is one who protects his subjects not only from external enemies but also poverty and hunger.'

Unlike many of his contemporaries, Shivaji was a fair and just ruler. He prioritised his people's welfare over everything else, even his own ego. And it wouldn't be an exaggeration to say that his people lived in stability and prosperity during his reign.

POWER THROUGH POLICIES

The reason for this is Shivaji Maharaj's administrative know-how and execution. There was forethought and deliberation behind each of his rules, regulations and policies. Although a lot has been said about Shivaji's daring adventures, courage, cunning and military strategy, not enough has been said about his pragmatism and administrative expertise.

DELEGATION OF AUTHORITY

In his earliest days as a leader, even as a 17-year-old with his new team of chieftains, Shivaji was in favour of delegation. His first council was made up of a *peshwa* (prime minister), *majumdar* (accountant), *dabir* (foreign minister) and *sachiv* (secretary). As his territory grew, he expanded his ministry to the much-renowned *ashta pradhan* committee which also included a *senapati* (commander in chief), *waqnavis* (interior minister), *nyayadhish* (chief justice) and panditrao (chief priest). Shivaji was uneducated and relied on the advice of his ministers to understand the intricacies of his policies. Although Shivaji always ran a tight ship, these ministers had reasonable understanding and control over their portfolios which meant that the administration could go on smoothly even if the king and his army were busy with a military campaign at any given time.

MONTHLY SALARY FOR SOLDIERS

In the first few months of forming his army, Shivaji formalised the practice of paying a monthly salary to his soldiers. This practice was quite unlike that of other kings or chieftains of the time. In those days, typically, after a successful campaign and annexation, a king would gift land or *jagir* to an army chief to manage and earn revenue from as reward for fighting on his behalf. This led to a lot of corruption and mismanagement of revenue in the kingdom. Besides this, the soldiers lower in the ranks would keep a portion of the loot from enemy territory as reward. Although this worked as a reward for the men, their families at home would suffer from poverty. However, this system led to needless violence and deaths of thousands of innocent civilians. Shivaji Maharaj realised that the Mavlas who first joined his army were actually farmers tilling their land. If the young man in the household was away fighting a battle, who would till the land? If there was no one to till the land, how would the family feed itself? By giving these men a monthly salary, Shivaji ensured that the families wouldn't go hungry. The other advantage of this policy was that the treasure and money looted from enemy territory went straight to the king's official treasury and was used for the betterment of the kingdom and its public.

MILITARY RULES AND REGULATIONS

Shivaji also instituted many military rules and regulations. Being of short height, in the first few years of military training itself, Shivaji realised that smaller, heavy swords put him at a disadvantage. He always used long, slim and light swords which were easy to wield. He then ensured that most of his soldiers used these swords so as to have maximum impact on the enemy. Another weapon he favoured was the traditional *dandpatta*, a long blade of metallic ribbon. This blade shivered and rippled unpredictably when flung during attack and required considerable skill while wielding. It ended up causing maximum harm to the enemy.

An expert in *ganimikawa,* Shivaji knew that stealth and speed were of prime importance. That is why he only used horses in his army instead of slower animals like elephants or camels like his enemies did. Horses operated efficiently on all the steep hills and forests that Shivaji excelled in attacking from.

AUSTERITY, ALWAYS

Shivaji Maharaj was not a man unduly given to luxuries and material possessions. Because of this, he discouraged indulgences by his soldiers as well. It is said that his soldiers were not allowed to carry too many comforts like mattresses during their battles in foreign territory.

Language of power

Shivaji Maharaj believed that language had great power. He was of the opinion that Swarajya would be truly elusive and unachievable till his people took pride in using their own language. Another practice that the Chhatrapati institutionalised was the abolition of Persian (Pharsi) and Arabic languages in official dealings and transactions and usage of Marathi and Sanskrit in all official administrative processes. This also helped in unifying people under the aegis of the Maratha empire.

RESPECT FOR WOMEN

Shivaji Maharaj followed these policies to the T even during peace time. His punishment for crimes committed against women were quite harsh.

The other rule Shivaji Maharaj had instituted, unlike other kings of his stature, was that women or kids were not to be taken captive. If innocent civilians were captured during battle or looting, they were all released unconditionally after the battle.

This rule originated from Jijabai's tutelage that all women were to be respected and all children to be protected at all costs. Jijabai believed that women and children were the fulcrum of every society. It was they who suffered the most in times of insecurity and war and therefore, should not have to suffer indignity as well. There are several examples of Shivaji releasing women and child prisoners and penalising his own soldiers who captured them in vengeance. As in the Hirkani legend, Shivaji was very upset that a working woman was not allowed to get home to her child. And while he did not relax his rule of closing the fort's doors at sunset, he did instruct his security to relax the rules in extenuating circumstances.

INCLUSIVITY AND TOLERANCE

Jijabai was an extremely spiritual woman. When Shivaji was but a child, Jijabai would often visit temples, Sufi dargahs, Sikh gurudwaras, saintly men and attend *kirtans* and other devotional gatherings with him. She truly believed that all human beings were equal and treated everyone with respect. Shivaji emulated the same principles in his life too. In fact, his army included men of all castes and religions, dedicated to fighting for their motherland. When the expanse of his territory grew, Shivaji also specially recruited skilled soldiers from Mughal, Adil Shahi and Rajputana armies to learn about enemy operations and strategy. This helped Maratha soldiers stay abreast with information about the enemy and often enabled them to plan guerilla attacks at quick notice. The other advantage of this was the secular and inclusive nature of Shivaji's army and administration, which, in turn, did not discriminate against any caste, community or religion.

This is why when Mughal Emperor Aurangzeb announced the *jiziya* tax against his Hindu subjects, Shivaji Maharaj took it upon himself to advise him to discontinue the discriminatory practice.

An excerpt from the letter that the Chhatrapati wrote to Emperor Aurangzeb after he announced the *jiziya* tax in his kingdom, reads:

'It has recently come to my ears that, on the grounds of the war with me having exhausted your wealth and emptied your treasury, your Majesty has ordered that money under the name of jiziya should be collected from the Hindus and imperial needs supplied with it. May it please your Majesty! That architect of the fabric of **your** *empire, [Jalaluddin] Akbar Padishah, reigned with full power for 52 [lunar] years. He adopted the admirable policy of universal harmony (sulh-i-kul) in relation to all the various sects, such as Christians, Jews, Muslims, Dadu's followers, sky-worshippers (falakia), malakia, materialists (ansaria), atheists (daharia), Brahmans and Jain priests. The aim of his liberal heart was to cherish and protect all the people. So, he became famous under the title of Jagat-Guru, "the World's spiritual guide".*

Next, the Emperor Nuruddin Jahangir, for 22 years, spread his gracious shade on the head of the world and its dwellers, gave his heart to his friends and his hand to his work, and gained his desires. The Emperor Shah Jahan, for 32 years, cast his blessed shade on the head of the world and gathered the fruit of eternal life — which is only a synonym for **they,** *too, had the power of levying the jiziya; but they did not give place to bigotry in their hearts, as they considered all men, high and low, created by God to be [living] examples of the nature of diverse creeds and temperaments. May it please your Majesty! If you believe in the true Divine Book and Word of God (i.e., the*

Quran), you will find there [that God is styled] Rabbul-alamin, the Lord of all men, and not Rabb~ul~musalmin, the Lord of the Muhammadans only.

To show bigotry for any man's creed and practices is equivalent to altering the words of the Holy Book. To draw new lines on a picture is equivalent to finding fault with the painter. Apart from its injustice, this imposition of the jiziya is an innovation in India and inexpedient.

How can the royal spirit permit you to add the hardship of the jiziya to this grievous state of things? The infamy will quickly spread from west to east and become recorded in books of history that the Emperor of Hindustan, covering the beggars' bowls, takes jiziya from Brahmans and Jain monks, yogis, sannyāsis, bairāgis, paupers, mendicants, ruined wretches, and the famine-stricken, that his valour is shown by attacks on the wallets of beggars, that he dashes down to the ground the name and honour of the Timurids!'

Emperor Aurangzeb did not acknowledge or respond to this correspondence sent by Shivaji Maharaj. However, the letter is proof of Shivaji's world view, inclusivity and tolerance of spirit. This is a prime example of what present-day leaders can learn about religious tolerance in a multi-faith society such as India.

Whether it was his military acumen; his daring pursuits; his administrative know-how or his sheer popularity among his people, Chhatrapati Shivaji Maharaj was a leader like no other.

Today, when we speak of the Great Chhatrapati Shivaji Maharaj, let us not forget Jijabai's young Shivba who dared to dream and took those first long strides towards Swarajya. Today, whether it is Maharashtra's fields, its forts, its seas, its people—each and every person who believes in his legacy, ideals and the dream to make Maharashtra great— they all echo the same cry.

Shivba ... Shivaji! You made Maharashtra proud!

Also by the Author